Childhood
Sexual Abuse

Developmental Clinical Psychology and Psychiatry Series

Series Editor: Alan E. Kazdin, Yale University

Recent volumes in this series . . .

Childhood Sexual Abuse

An Evidence Based Perspective

David M. Fergusson
Paul E. Mullen

Volume 40
Developmental Clinical Psychology and Psychiatry

St. Petersburg
Junior College

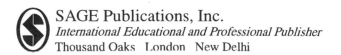
SAGE Publications, Inc.
International Educational and Professional Publisher
Thousand Oaks London New Delhi

For information:

SAGE Publications, Inc.
2455 Teller Road
Thousand Oaks, California 91320
E-mail: order@sagepub.com

SAGE Publications Ltd.
6 Bonhill Street
London EC2A 4PU
United Kingdom

SAGE Publications India Pvt. Ltd.
M-32 Market
Greater Kailash I
New Delhi 110 048 India

Printed in the United States of America

Library of Congress Cataloging-in-Publication Data

Fergusson, David Murray, 1944–
    Childhood sexual abuse: An evidence-based perspective / by
David M. Fergusson, Paul E. Mullen.
        p. cm.—(Developmental clinical psychology and psychiatry
series; v. 40)
    Includes bibliographical references and index.
    ISBN 0-7619-1136-7 (acid-free paper)
    ISBN 0-7619-1137-5 (pbk.: acid-free paper)
    1. Child sexual abuse. 2. Sexually abused children.
3. Evidence-based medicine. 4. Child psychopathology.
I. Mullen, Paul E. II. Title. III. Series: Developmental
clinical psychology and psychiatry; v. 40.
    RJ507.S49 F47   1999
    616.85'836—dc21   98-51234

99 00 01 02 03 04 05 7 6 5 4 3 2 1

Acquisition Editor: Jim Nageotte
Editorial Assistant: Heidi Van Middlesworth
Production Editor: Denise Santoyo
Editorial Assistant: Stephanie Allen
Typesetter: Lynn Miyata
Cover Designer: Candice Harman
Indexer: Teri Greenberg

CONTENTS

SERIES EDITOR'S INTRODUCTION

Interest in child development and adjustment is by no means new. Yet, only recently has the study of children benefited from advances in both clinical and scientific research. Advances in the social and biological sciences, the emergence of disciplines and subdisciplines that focus exclusively on childhood and adolescence, and a greater appreciation of the impact of such influences as the family, peers, and school have helped accelerate research on developmental psychopathology. Apart from interest in the study of child development and adjustment for its own sake, the need to address clinical problems that occur in adulthood naturally draws one to investigate precursors in childhood and adolescence.

Within a relatively brief period, the study of psychopathology among children and adolescents has proliferated considerably. Several different professional journals, annual book series, and handbooks devoted entirely to the study of children, adolescents, and their adjustment document the proliferation of work in the field. Nevertheless, there is a paucity of resource material that presents information in an authoritative, systematic, and disseminable fashion. There is a need within the field to convey the latest developments and to represent different disciplines, approaches, and conceptual views to the topics of childhood and adolescent adjustment and maladjustment.

The Sage Series **Developmental Clinical Psychology and Psychiatry** is designed to serve uniquely several needs of the field. The Series encompasses individual monographs prepared by experts in the fields of clinical child psychology, child psychiatry, child development, and related disciplines. The primary focus is on developmental psychopathology, which refers broadly here to the diagnosis, assessment, treatment, and prevention of problems that arise in the period from infancy through adolescence. A working assumption of the Series is that understanding, identifying, and treating problems of youth must draw on multiple disciplines and diverse views within a given discipline.

The task for individual contributors is to present the latest theory and research on various topics, including specific types of dysfunction, diagnostic and treatment approaches, and special problem areas that affect adjustment. Core topics within clinical work are addressed by the Series. Authors are asked to bridge potential theory, research, and clinical practice, and to outline the current status and future directions of these disciplines. The goals of the Series and the tasks presented to individual contributors are demanding. We have been extremely fortunate in recruiting leaders in the fields who have been able to translate their recognized scholarship and expertise into highly readable works on contemporary topics.

The present book, by Drs. David Fergusson and Paul Mullen, examines the scope, nature, and effects of child sexual abuse. Central areas are covered, including evidence on the prevalence of child abuse, characteristics of abused children and perpetrators of abuse, the short- and long-term impact of abuse, and treatment. The authors draw from psychiatric epidemiology and developmental psychopathology and a range of research methods, including survey research and controlled clinical trials. An incisive account of the research is used to convey precisely what is and is not known about abuse and how current findings are in keeping with or depart from debates about the nature of abuse. Balanced coverage is provided on such controversial topics as the role of child abuse in contributing to psychiatric disorders, the utility and verifiability of information obtained from child testimony, and recovery of memories or false memories of child abuse. The experience of the authors in years of research on child abuse has provided them with a grasp of the theory, research, and clinical and social issues that is without peer. This book provides an authoritative, thoroughly informed, and incisive examination of the topic.

ALAN E. KAZDIN, PHD
Series Editor

ACKNOWLEDGMENTS

We would like to acknowledge the work and diligence of Drs. Michael Lynskey and Lianne Woodward for their assistance in the preparation and editing of this book. Without their efforts and assistance, the task of preparing the work would have been far more onerous than it proved to be. Thanks are also due to Judith Stone, Kerry Purcell, and Julie King for their efforts in typing successive drafts of the manuscript and for the care with which they approached this task.

1

A HISTORICAL PERSPECTIVE

The knowledge that children are on occasion subjected to sexual abuse is not new, and neither are attempts to study such abuse systematically (Hamilton, 1929; Kinsey, Pomeroy, Martin, & Gebhadt, 1953; Landis et al., 1940; Simpson, 1988). What is new is the widespread public awareness of child sexual abuse (CSA) as an all too common event in the lives of children and a belief that such experiences are not only distressing at the time but that they can produce long-term damage and disturbance. The sexual abuse of children is no longer regarded merely as a vice and a product of evil acts, as it was in the 19th century. It has come to be viewed variously as an infringement on the rights of children; a gross example of patriarchal domination and exploitation; a social challenge; a cause of mental disorders; an explanation of personal and social failings; a challenge to existing legal processes; and the basis for burgeoning industries in protection, detection, and victim therapy. CSA has become one of the defining cultural themes of our age, so much so that it is all too easy to lose sight of the individual victims of abuse, in the midst of the sound and fury generated around the topic of CSA.

In this book, we attempt to provide a critical and, as far as possible, impartial assessment of the evidence about a range of issues that have dominated the contemporary debates around CSA. These issues include the prevalence of CSA (Chapter 2), the characteristics of CSA victims and perpetrators (Chapter 3), the effects of CSA on children (Chapter 4), and the effects of CSA on adults (Chapter 5). Our general aim has been to review these areas, ascertaining the goodness of fit between commonly held assumptions about CSA and the available evidence. An important subtext of this analysis is the highlighting of methodological and epistemological issues that arise in the study of CSA. This review emphasizes the need for caution in interpreting a complex body of evidence that is fraught with uncertainty and amenable to multiple interpretations.

1

Inevitably, this analysis will lead us to a position that will disappoint the more enthusiastic advocates of some of the more radical positions in the CSA discourse. This book suggests, however, that although CSA may not be as widespread or damaging as implied in some advocacy-based accounts of this area, neither is it as uncommon or harmless as implied by overly skeptical views of this area. We hope to show that the weight of the evidence reveals that exposure to CSA is a not uncommon childhood experience that often, but not invariably, has damaging short- and long-term consequences.

To set the background for this work, the present chapter provides a brief account of the historical context within which contemporary concerns and research about CSA have developed.

PROLOGUE

The sexual abuse of children has been discovered and rediscovered throughout history (Olafson, Corwin, & Summit, 1993). One of the more influential rediscoveries was that of Freud (1896), who initially concluded that many of his patients had been molested or victimized during childhood. On the basis of these observations, Freud formulated his seduction theory, in which he identified child sexual abuse as a major etiological factor in neurosis. This hypothesis was relatively short-lived since Freud abandoned this seduction theory in favor of the Oedipal theory, and accounts of CSA were relegated to being childhood fantasies rather than descriptions of reality (see Chapter 5 for a more detailed account of Freud's position).

During the first half of the 20th century, there was relatively little interest in the topic of CSA, despite the publication of several surveys in the 1940s and 1950s (Landis et al., 1940; Kinsey et al., 1953) that indicated a substantial prevalence of CSA (Green, 1993). It has been suggested that the lack of professional interest in CSA was due to reports of CSA being either discounted as fantasy or reconstructed as behaviors that were not harmful to children (Olafson et al., 1993).

In the early 1960s, there was a rediscovery of the problem of physical abuse of children as a result of the pioneering work of Kempe and his associates on the battered child syndrome (Kempe, Silverman, Steele, Droegemueller, & Silver, 1962). That research set in motion increasing interest and concern about the physical abuse of children. However, it was not until a decade later that attention once again focused on the issue of CSA.

CHILDHOOD SEXUAL ABUSE: 1970-2000

Scott (1995) has suggested that the history of the rediscovery of CSA in the late 20th century can be represented by four stages; discovery, diffusion, consolidation, and reification, which can broadly be organized into a series of epochs.

The (Re)discovery of CSA: 1970-1980

The initial impetus for contemporary concerns about CSA was provided by accounts of adult women reporting on their personal experiences of CSA (Armstrong, 1978; Butler, 1978; Rush, 1974, 1980; Russell, 1986). These accounts were often directly, or indirectly, linked to themes emerging from the women's movement. At this time, the primary focus of concern was with father–daughter incest rather than with the broader issue of CSA.

Important in this rediscovery of CSA as a social problem was that the voice of the sexually abused child was largely that of an adult recalling her victimization and describing the impact of CSA on her life. This process contrasted sharply with the way in which the problem of childhood physical abuse had been rediscovered a decade earlier. At that time, health professionals described the abuse, medicalized that abuse, and took on the role of advocating for the victims to such an extent that the voice of the physically abused child became that of the physician and the child-care worker; now, however, the voice of the sexually abused child belonged to the adult survivor and, through her, to the women's movement and the therapist.

The different contexts within which childhood physical abuse and childhood sexual abuse were rediscovered were to be reflected in their subsequent histories. To a large extent, concerns about childhood physical abuse have continued to be founded in professional and largely clinical concerns about the identification, treatment, and management of abuse. In contrast, models of CSA and its management have remained closely aligned with issues of the politics of gender and the politics of victimization.

The advantage of the largely adulto-centric agendas that characterized the rediscovery of CSA was due to the active role played by persons who had themselves been victims of abuse. The result was an immediate acquisition of a wider context in which to place debates about sexual abuse than had been the case for child physical abuse. The victims of CSA could speak for themselves and, to some extent, direct the narrative that gave meaning to their abuse so that they could at least compete with professionals and scientists in shaping the discourse on CSA. The central role played by adult victims had real benefits both in shaping empirical research and in driving social policy. However, this adulto-centric perspective also contributed to a disparity between the social energy and the financial resources that were devoted to treating adult survivors, as compared to the protection and treatment of abused children.

Hindsight enables one to see the manner in which CSA was rediscovered in the 1970s and why this discovery had such a powerful impact on cultural constructions of power, male sexuality, and the nature of victimization. These origins also provide insights into some of the problems that have continued to bedevil the field. Central to the discovery of CSA was the assumption that adults could adequately recall their childhood experiences in a way that realistically reflected the events of childhood. The key role of recall in defining CSA can now be seen as, on the one hand, encouraging overly skeptical attitudes about reports of CSA and, on the other hand, encouraging uncritical acceptance of the validity of recalled experience.

The result was that by the end of the 1970s, the rediscovery of CSA had led to a body of evidence and theory that was largely based on the accounts of adult female survivors of CSA, with the validity of these accounts being underwritten by a growing body of feminist theories that regarded CSA as one of the manifestations of those patriarchal social structures that oppressed women. These themes are captured in the comments of Herman (1981):

> It is not possible to write dispassionately about incest. The subject is entirely enmeshed not only in myth and folklore, but also in ideology. We have found that a frankly feminist perspective offers the best explanation of the existing data. Without an understanding of male supremacy and female oppression, it is impossible to explain why the vast majority of incest perpetrators (uncles, older brothers, stepfathers, and fathers) are male, and why the majority of victims (nieces, younger sisters, and daughters) are female. Without a feminist analysis, one is at a loss to explain why the reality of incest was for so long suppressed by supposedly responsible professional investigators, why public discussion of the subject awaited the women's liberation movement, or why the recent apologists for incest have been popular men's magazines. (p. 3)

Diffusion: 1980–1990

The rediscovery of CSA in the 1970s laid the foundations for the diffusion of knowledge about CSA to the general public that occurred predominantly in the 1980s. In this process, CSA was actively presented to the public, policymakers, and professionals as being sufficiently prevalent, sufficiently damaging, and sufficiently important to be seen as a problem of major social significance. The sympathies of the media were engaged by the problem of CSA, and it began to receive increasing attention (Haugaard & Reppucci, 1988; McDevitt, 1996). Over this period, a number of women's magazines ran stories about CSA and also began to poll their readers, usually through voluntary questionnaires, about their personal experiences of CSA.

Two features permeated this phase of the diffusion of knowledge about CSA. The first was that the definition of CSA tended to become increasingly broad and to encompass a wide range of unwanted childhood sexual experiences, ranging from exposure to indecent behavior to brutal and repeated rape. Parallel with this broadening of the definition of CSA were stories featured in the media that implied that a substantial portion of the female population were victims of CSA. These presentations gave the impression to many members of the public that large numbers of children were exposed to serious sexual assault, with these assaults being committed by family members, usually the father.

The growing awareness of CSA as an issue led to greater professional and scientific involvement, particularly with regard to the role of CSA in the genesis of mental health problems (Haugaard & Reppucci, 1988; Olafson et al., 1993). On occasion, the enthusiasm of professionals led to the over-zealous ascertainment of CSA and the pursuit of putative abusers. An example of these difficulties was provided by an investigation of CSA cases in the Cleveland Health District of Great Britain (Butler-Sloss, 1988). Attention had focused on Cleveland as a result of a localized epidemic in which over 120 children were diagnosed as being subject to CSA over a 6-month period. Most of these allegations of CSA were traceable to the work of two Cleveland pediatricians who had formed the strong, but spurious, opinion that the presence of anal dilatation (the atypical opening of the anus on clinical examination) provided strong physical evidence of CSA. The official report of the judicial inquiry into these events concluded that the epidemic of CSA allegations was, in part, due to overzealous and uncritical practice by the pediatricians involved. Similar events in other Western countries evoked concerns about the extent to which strong allegations of CSA were being based on evidence that was weak, flawed, or open to alternative interpretation (Ceci & Bruck, 1995; Green, 1986). Benedek and Schetky (1987a) noted,

> Child psychiatrists, paediatricians and mental health professionals have recently been concerned by a deluge of referrals requesting evaluation of young children in regard to allegations of sexual abuse. A new cottage industry/profession has evolved and a group of experts in this specialist area have emerged to fill a

serious need. Many of these experts, although well meaning, seem to be self-proclaimed and biased, always finding sexual abuse where alleged. (p. 912)

The occasionally overzealous pursuit of CSA was one of the products of the view that was widely promulgated in the 1980s that large numbers of children were the victims of serious sexual assault; in part, this was encouraged by the belief that in cases of CSA the child should always be believed (Ceci & Bruck, 1993), and in part it was a result of the understandable wish to give precedence to the protection of children over evidential issues. These views reflected the teething problems of an emerging area of care, treatment, and inquiry, but the net result was to create a social and intellectual climate during the 1980s that encouraged the use of weak evidence to make strong allegations of CSA.

Up until the 1980s, the general scientific research community had remained aloof from claims about the prevalence of CSA and generally approached these claims with considerable skepticism (Herman, 1981; Haugaard & Reppucci, 1988; Russell, 1986). However, with the growing public awareness of the issues raised by CSA, there was an exponential increase in research in this area, with researchers seeking to verify and examine claims about the prevalence of CSA, the social context within which CSA occurred, and the consequences of CSA for personal adjustment. Initial studies in this area were confined to relatively small and selected patient samples, but with the passage of time an increasing number of large-scale studies of CSA were conducted in the general population, which examined the prevalence, correlates, and consequences of CSA (Green, 1993).

Consideration of the methods by which knowledge about CSA was diffused in the 1980s suggests that this process led to both benefits and costs. The clear benefits were that the often dramatic ways in which issues of CSA were presented led to a rising public, professional, and political awareness of the social importance of this issue and of the pressing need to find ways and means of addressing this problem. As was the case with the rediscovery of CSA, the credit for bringing CSA to public and professional attention largely goes to advocacy groups who, in the face of often considerable skepticism, continued to insist that CSA was a common and neglected issue for both children and women. On the debit side of the ledger, the need to disseminate information about CSA to a largely skeptical public led to claims of CSA being stated in ways that may have exaggerated the extent of some aspects of the problem. In addition, the climate that resulted from claims about the prevalence of CSA and its psychological sequelae encouraged, in at least some instances, overly zealous professional attempts to identify CSA and CSA perpetrators.

Consolidation/Reification: 1990–2000

Toward the end of the 1980s, sufficient research and other evidence existed to provide compelling support for three general conclusions about CSA. First, that exposure to unwanted sexual experience during childhood was by no means uncommon. Second, that children reared in certain social or family circumstances were at increased risk of CSA. Third, that exposure to CSA in childhood was associated with increased risks of mental health and adjustment problems in both the early years and in later life. These conclusions led to a growing awareness that CSA victims had the right to therapy, support, and redress for their victimization, which, in turn, fostered the development of services and systems that specifically catered to the needs of victims of CSA.

Parallel to the consolidation of knowledge about CSA have been shifts in the direction and emphasis of research. In particular, the research literature of the 1980s was either dominated by studies of the prevalence of CSA in both the general population and selected clinical populations or else preoccupied with documenting the extent of adjustment difficulties among those reporting CSA. These emphases have begun to shift, with research moving increasingly toward issues concerned with measuring and classifying CSA or with the development of more refined methods for testing hypotheses about the effects of CSA on adults and children. One result of this consolidation process was to lay the foundations of a burgeoning sexual abuse industry that would be able to meet the needs of persons who had been sexually abused (Goodyear-Smith, 1993). This, in turn, has led to a proliferation of claims about the need to treat CSA as well as questions about whether existing therapies can meet those needs. Despite a very large investment in these methods and therapies to date, relatively little is known about the efficacy of CSA treatments. Existing trends in the research literature suggest that over the coming decade, research will increasingly focus on the extent to which CSA therapies can deliver what they claim to deliver (see Chapters 4 and 5).

In his discussion of the history of CSA, Scott (1995) notes that the final stage of the process of rediscovery involves reification. Reification refers to changes whereby a fluid social process becomes solidified into a rigid construct whose general properties and features remain beyond doubt or question. It is clear that CSA has yet to become a fully reified construct, but the early signs of rigidity and elevation to a social verity are obvious. One sign of this process of reification is the complete ease with which present-day journalists, politicians, and professionals speak of CSA, assuming that it exists as an easily recognizable object out there in the world, with its defining features known to all. Yet what constitutes CSA is still far from clear, and where the boundaries are to be placed is open to considerable debate.

One primary purpose of this book is to take stock of the evidence on the prevalence, causes, and consequences of CSA to examine the goodness of fit between the themes that have dominated public debates about CSA over a period of three decades compared to the available evidence. However, before undertaking this evaluation, we must address a number of issues relating to the conceptualization of CSA and views of its evidence.

CONCEPTUAL MATTERS

The Definition of CSA

The tendency for the concept of CSA to be reified has led to a situation in which CSA is treated as though it were a recognizable syndrome, like measles, that can be identified by the presence of a number of more or less objective and invariant signs and symptoms. However, the definition of CSA does not rest on objective signs and symptoms but, rather, on normative judgments. In general, the process of measuring and defining CSA involves two stages. In the first stage, evidence is gathered (usually by retrospective reports) about childhood sexual experiences and, particularly, unwanted sexual experiences. These accounts are then evaluated against some explicit, or implicit, normative standard to determine the extent to which the reported experience can be classified as abusive. Two features of this process are worthy of note:

- *Heterogeneity among those who have been classified as sexually abused.* Since the definition of CSA relies upon a normative judgment about acceptable and unacceptable childhood sexual experiences, it is clear that because of the heterogeneity of these experiences those persons classified as exposed to CSA do not comprise a homogeneous population who were exposed to a common set of childhood experiences. Rather, this group will represent an hetero-geneous group of individuals who are linked only by the fact that they have been exposed to sexual behaviors and sexual contact in childhood that are deemed, by some standard, to be inappropriate and socially unacceptable. However, these experiences in childhood may range from reports of a single incident of seeing a man expose himself indecently to reports of severe and multiple sexual assaults. This heterogeneity in the classification of CSA poses major difficulties in interpreting estimates of the prevalence of CSA, to the extent that these estimates may be inflated, by including children who were exposed to non-physically intrusive episodes of abuse, or reduced, by including only severe incidents of sexual assault (Haugaard & Reppucci, 1988).

- *Indeterminacies in the criteria for defining abuse.* Extensive literature exists that identifies, in various ways, criteria that demarcate children who are sexually abused from those who are not. Although this literature provides a useful account of various bases for defining abuse, its value is limited by the failure of many writers to recognize that there is not, and cannot be, a single universal definition of CSA. Such a definition would require that reports of childhood sexual experiences be evaluated against a generally accepted set of normative and moral standards that determines which acts are classified as abusive and which are not. No such gold standard exists. Rather, there is a spectrum of opinion ranging from those definitions that consider any unseemly sexual experience in childhood to be abuse to those definitions that argue that many of the incidents commonly described as CSA are, in fact, beneficial and welcomed by children (Yates, 1978).

The most straightforward way of addressing the definition of CSA is to move away from conceptualizations that reify CSA as a clearly defined syndrome and move toward approaches that deconstruct the notion of CSA to describe different types of unwanted and potentially harmful sexual experiences to which children are exposed. For example, it is perfectly possible to ask the question "How does the experience of being confronted by an adult who indecently exposes himself influence the psychological health and well-being of children in both the short and long term?" without engaging in a debate over whether or not such behavior is sexually abusive. Indeed, the judgment about whether or not indecent exposure is a sexually abusive act is likely to depend considerably on the extent to which it can be shown that such exposure has harmful or distressing effects for children.

For these reasons, research into childhood sexual abuse has begun to move away from definitions that aggregate a diverse set of childhood experiences into a general category of CSA, and toward accounts that describe the nature, extent, and intrusiveness of unwanted sexual experiences in childhood and how these experiences may affect children and adults (Anderson, Martin, Mullen, Romans, & Herbison, 1993; Fergusson, Horwood, & Lynskey, 1996; Haugaard & Emery, 1989; Mullen, Martin, Anderson, Romans, & Herbison, 1993). As we will show later (Chapters 4 and 5), the evidence points to the view that the acts and behaviors that have been classified as CSA vary from the mild to the very severe, with this spectrum being reflected in the extent to which the individual shows evidence of harmful effects attributable to these acts.

The Place of Epidemiological Research in the Study of CSA

The historical processes underlying the rediscovery of CSA in the latter part of the 20th century have resulted in a situation in which knowledge and opinion about this area has come from three rather different types of discourse—from the accounts of CSA survivors in reporting on their experiences of CSA and the ways in which these experiences shaped their lives and influenced their personal happiness, adjustment, and well-being; from the accounts of clinicians who have reported on their patients' experiences of CSA and described the ways in which these experiences have led to adjustment difficulties; and from the results of population-based epidemiological research in which researchers have described the prevalence of CSA in population samples and have examined the statistical linkages between CSA exposures and measures of individual adjustment.

Each of these accounts gives, or may give, rather different perspectives on the issue of CSA, and all are strongly discriminated by the degree to which reports about CSA may be generalized. In general, survivor accounts illustrate (a) that CSA occurs and (b) that such childhood experiences may have a large impact on individual adjustment and well-being. However, such accounts fail to address issues of the prevalence of CSA in the population and, more important, the extent to which the experiences recounted by CSA survivors are typical of the experiences of all children who have been exposed to CSA. Furthermore, accounts of CSA survivors may also be influenced by the opinions, attitudes, and values of those individuals in their attempt to reconstruct the experience of CSA and thereby give meaning to this experience in the context of their lives and life experiences.

Clinician reports of CSA provide accounts that are of greater generality than those provided by CSA survivors since, typically, these accounts attempt to distill and summarize the common features of a series of cases of CSA that come to the attention of the clinician. In this approach, clinician accounts tend to emphasize features that are common to cases of CSA rather than focus on the specific, and perhaps idiosyncratic, features of a single case. However, clinician accounts are limited in that they may contain an overrepresentation of individuals who develop difficulties following their exposure to CSA and may also be restricted to more severe cases of CSA that have psychiatric sequelae.

To a large extent, epidemiological research into CSA reflects an attempt to overcome the sampling limitations that are present in both the accounts of individual CSA survivors and the accounts of clinicians. Typically, epidemiological research will focus on three key issues:

1. Prevalence: What fraction of the population is exposed to CSA, and what is the extent of variation in the CSA experiences reported by population members?
2. Correlates/predictors: What factors distinguish between those individuals who are exposed to CSA and those who are not?
3. Consequences: To what extent does exposure to CSA have long- and short-term effects on individual adjustment and well-being, taking into account (a) the nature of the abuse being reported and (b) other characteristics of those reporting abuse?

These questions are typically addressed by taking relatively large and representative samples of a given population in which reports of CSA, the social and personal context within which CSA occurred, and the psychiatric symptoms displayed by both those reporting CSA and those not reporting CSA are gathered. The output of such research is a series of statistical propositions that describe (a) the relative frequency with which CSA is reported; (b) the social, demographic, and other characteristics that are associated with increased risks of CSA; and (c) the extent to which reports of CSA are associated with increased risks of psychiatric symptoms and other adjustment problems.

Each of these approaches has strengths and limitations. The accounts of CSA survivors have the valuable feature of placing CSA in the context of the life experiences of a specific individual and of showing the ways in which exposure to CSA has colored and influenced his or her life course. Clinician accounts describe the features of CSA victims in the context of clinical practice. Epidemiological research describes the statistical properties of CSA within a given population and is useful for making judgments about the prevalence of CSA in the population and the extent to which CSA experiences have, on average, harmful effects on population members. However, such accounts are also limited, as they render the potentially rich accounts of life experiences into statistical abstractions.

The clear conclusion of this line of argument is that the choice of approach to assessing the issue of CSA depends very much on the purposes for which the account is to be used. If one's concern is to provide an in-depth account of CSA from the standpoint of the individuals who experienced CSA or from the standpoint of the clinician dealing with the issues faced by CSA victims, then the personal and case history material form the richest source of information. If, however, one's concern is to move beyond the individual case or the individual clinical practice to describe the problem of CSA in the context of a given population of individuals, then epidemiological research will provide the most appropriate account.

In this book, we present a largely epidemiological perspective on the issue of CSA. There are two major reasons for adopting this perspective. The first is our view that a strong foundation has been laid of qualitative research based on personal and clinical accounts of CSA experiences. The second reason for the predominantly epidemiological emphasis of this book is that over the past three decades there has been an increasing growth in epidemiological studies of CSA that have looked at the prevalence, correlates, and consequences of CSA (Green, 1993). Given this ever expanding body of research, it is useful to take stock of existing evidence in order to examine the conclusions that may be drawn from this evidence as well as the issues that arise in the interpretation of the available evidence. More generally, what we hope to describe is the degree of certainty and doubt that exists in contemporary epidemiological evidence on the issue of CSA.

2

THE PREVALENCE OF SEXUAL ABUSE DURING CHILDHOOD

The proportion of the child population who are exposed to sexual abuse is a source of ongoing debate and controversy (Bagley, 1990; Feldman et al., 1991; Finkelhor, 1994; Kinsey et al., 1953; Peters, Wyatt, & Finkelhor, 1986). Although statistics have been available for many years on the number of CSA cases that are known to welfare agencies and are reported to the police, such information does not accurately describe the prevalence of CSA within the community, owing to the fact that the majority of CSA cases fail to reach official attention (Finkelhor, 1994). Officially recorded cases of CSA in the United States showed a tenfold increase from 1976 to 1983 (Finkelhor, 1984), but it is likely this apparent increase can be attributed to rising public awareness and concerns over the issue of CSA rather than to an escalation in abuse. For these reasons, officially recorded statistics provide little clear guidance about either the prevalence of CSA or, indeed, time trends in CSA rates.

In this chapter, we present an overview of the prevalence of CSA as reported in recent studies, using both random community samples and samples of convenience, together with an analysis of the complex issues that arise when interpreting these estimates.

ASSESSMENT OF THE PREVALENCE OF ABUSE

In the analysis reported later in this chapter, we present estimates from a series of studies about the percentage of a given sample of individuals who report that they were sexually abused during childhood. This statistic has been variously described in the literature as the incidence or prevalence of childhood sexual abuse (Peters et al., 1986). In fact, it does not conform to the strict definition of either incidence or prevalence. The incidence of a condition refers to the rate of occurrence of this condition per unit of time, whereas prevalence refers to the portion of the population who have the condition at a given time (Susser, 1973). Strictly, what is reported in most studies of CSA is the cumulative incidence of abuse over the period of childhood. Although this cumulative incidence is not strictly a prevalence, it has a similar interpretation to a prevalence estimate, reflecting the proportion of those who report or disclose exposure to childhood sexual abuse at a given time. For this reason, we have used the term *prevalence* as a convenient label to describe this statistic, on the understanding that what is meant by prevalence in this context is the fraction or percentage of the population who report that they have been exposed to sexual abuse at some time during their childhood.

Over the past 20 years, a growing number of studies have, in various ways, attempted to estimate the prevalence of childhood sexual abuse in unselected general population samples (for reviews, see Finkelhor, 1994; Peters et al., 1986). These studies have produced widely varying prevalence estimates that have ranged from 3% to 30% of males and from 6% to 62% of females (Peters et al., 1986). Nonetheless, typical prevalence estimates suggest that approximately 15% to 30% of females report exposure to sexual abuse or some form of unwanted sexual attention during childhood (see Tables 2.1 and 2.2). A variety of factors may explain the wide variability in estimates of the prevalence of childhood sexual abuse.

Variations in the Definition of CSA

Variations in the definition of CSA may lead to variations in estimates of prevalence. As we pointed out in Chapter 1, there are two general problems that may lead to variability in the definition of CSA. First, the normative basis on which CSA is defined means that there are no unique and universally agreed-on definitions of CSA that clearly demarcate between abused and nonabused children. Second, among those classified as being exposed to CSA, there is often considerable heterogeneity in the nature of the abuse incident to which children have been exposed. These two features have created a situation in which different investigations have adopted different criteria for the identification of CSA, with these variations being reflected in variations in prevalence estimates.

Definitions that seek to partition the population of children into those who have been sexually abused and those who have not been abused must invariably adopt arbitrary criteria about the extent of sexual intrusion, contact, coercion, and physical assault that may be classified as abusive, which leads to considerable variability in the resulting estimates of the prevalence of child abuse. One means of addressing these problems may be to avoid the use of global definitions of child abuse and instead classify children more precisely by the nature of the unwanted sexual experiences they encounter during childhood. This deconstruction of the global term *child sexual abuse* into the constituent elements is not only potentially demystifying, but it also allows for more effective and precise investigations into the impact of CSA on children in their early years as well as on their adult functioning.

Problems of Validity, Reliability, and Measurement

Studies of childhood sexual abuse in general population samples have relied on the retrospective reports of adults about their memories of events occurring during childhood. There are many problems to be faced in assessing the reliability and accuracy of such reports, and retrospectively reported childhood experiences may be subject to substantial fallibility arising from problems of recall (Henry, Moffitt, Caspi, Langley, & Silva, 1994; Squire, 1989), from a refusal or reluctance of those exposed to abuse to disclose these experiences (Haugaard & Emery, 1989; Peters et al., 1986), and, possibly, as a result of memories of painful childhood experiences being repressed (Fredrickson, 1992; Herman, 1992; Penfold, 1996). There is no obvious way in which the accuracy of reports of sexual abuse can be established because there is no external criterion against which most reports of CSA can be validated. It would appear that less than 10% of CSA cases ascertained in studies of adults were made known to authorities at the time of the abuse, and the majority of cases were not even reported to parents or other adults (Anderson et al., 1993; Fleming, 1997). This makes confirmation that is dependent on contemporary records overly restrictive. Perhaps the best hope of addressing these issues is through the use of longitudinal or panel studies in which the same individuals are questioned on multiple occasions about their child sexual abuse experiences to examine the consistency and stability with which abuse experiences are recounted (Bertolli, Morgenstern, & Sorenson, 1995). To date, few studies have examined this issue, but the existing literature suggests moderate-to-good consistency of CSA reports (Martin, Anderson, Romans, Mullen, & O'Shea, 1993).

Framing Questions about Abuse

In addition to the difficulties associated with the recall and disclosure of childhood sexual abuse, a number of more specific issues arise when questioning individuals about their experiences of child abuse. Growing evidence estimates that the prevalence of abuse will vary considerably, depending on the ways in which researchers make their inquiries (Dill, Chu, Grob, & Eisen, 1991; Martin et al., 1993; Peters et al., 1986). Approaches have ranged from relying on individuals' responses to a single survey item (e.g., Hibbard, Ingersoll, & Orr, 1990; Wellman, 1993) to using methods with multiple questions and means of assessment (e.g., Anderson et al., 1993). In general, it seems important to base inquiries about childhood sexual abuse on a comprehensive set of questions about childhood sexual experiences and relationships (Peters et al., 1986).

Reflection suggests that individuals who are questioned about sexual abuse are faced with the complex tasks of (a) reviewing their childhood history of sexual experiences and (b) reporting those experiences that meet explicit or implicit criteria for sexual abuse. It is likely that this process of recall and review will be assisted if questions about sexual abuse address specific aspects of each individual's childhood sexual experience rather than ask individuals about their exposure to sexual abuse experiences in general (Carlin et al., 1994; Martin et al., 1993; Peters et al., 1986).

Not only may the reporting of sexual abuse be influenced by the method of framing the questions about childhood sexual experiences, but there have also been suggestions that the method by which data are gathered will influence disclosure (Dill et al., 1991; Martin et al., 1993; Peters et al., 1986). There are three commonly employed methods of ascertainment. A number of studies, particularly those on college students, have used anonymous self-report questionnaires (e.g., Briere, Smiljanich, & Henschel, 1994; Peters & Range, 1995). Other studies have conducted telephone interviewing surveys (e.g., Finkelhor, Hotaling, Lewis, & Smith, 1990; Finkelhor & Dziuba-Leatherman, 1994). Still others have used face-to-face interviews (e.g., Anderson et al., 1993; Fergusson et al., 1996). These methods differ in the extent to which they protect the privacy of the subject, with anonymous self-report measures providing the greatest protection and face-to-face interviews the least.

It has been suggested that methods that protect respondent privacy are likely to result in greater disclosure (Dill et al., 1991; Martin et al., 1993). The evidence in favor of this conclusion is equivocal, with some studies finding that methods that protect confidentiality improve disclosure (Dill et al., 1991; Martin et al., 1993), while others claim that more information is generated in face-to-face interviews (Peters et al., 1986).

In face-to-face or telephone interviews, the training and skill of the questioner is relevant. Disclosure will be encouraged by the interviewer's interpersonal skills and sensitivity, augmented by relevant training and supervision. The literature on childhood sexual abuse has paid little attention to the extent to which variations in interviewer training and interviewer characteristics may influence the reporting and disclosure of CSA. There is, however, evidence from a broader type of social survey literature that suggests that such factors play an influential role in determining responses to survey questions (Fowler & Mangione, 1989; Groves, 1989). One feature of interviewers that has been discussed is gender, and there have been claims that interviewers who are of the same gender as the respondent may encourage greater disclosure and more frank discussion of CSA episodes. The only study to make use of both male and female interviewers that reported on the influence of the interviewer's gender did not find any significant effect on respondents' disclosure (Siegel, Sorenson, Golding, Burnam, & Stein, 1987).

Sample Selection Factors

Sample selection may have a profound effect on prevalence estimates. This is evident from the studies that have reported on the prevalence of CSA based on participants drawn from such groups as attenders at psychiatric and child guidance clinics (e.g., Dell & Eisenhower, 1990), children coming to the attention of welfare agencies (e.g., Von Dadelszen, 1987), people coming to the notice of criminal justice systems (e.g., Dembo, Williams, Schmeidler, & Christensen, 1993), and adult psychiatric patients (e.g., Brown & Anderson, 1991; Chu & Dill, 1990). Frequently, although not invariably, such studies suggest a high prevalence of abuse, in which the majority of those questioned disclose some form of exposure to CSA. However, it would be unreasonable to believe that estimates of prevalence of CSA that are based on such samples reflect the prevalence of abuse in the population at large. This is because, with participants who are selected because of various personal or family difficulties and who are conspicuous because of these difficulties, it is likely that the CSA experiences and risks they face will be atypical and not representative of the general conditions that apply within the population at large.

The preferred way of assessing the prevalence of abuse is to obtain a representative sample of the population using random sampling methods and to assess for each member of the sample the extent of his or her exposure (if any) to CSA (Peters et al., 1986). Even with such a design, bias may influence estimates. One such source of bias may come from a nonresponse in survey investigations. Reasons for nonparticipation will include a failure to trace the individual, refusal of the individual to participate, or an inability to interview the individual because of language barriers or other difficulties.

To the extent that these sample losses are likely to be systematic, they may introduce bias into prevalence estimates (Haugaard & Emery, 1989; Peters et al., 1986). Such bias will occur if the processes by which sample members are lost to a study are associated with the individual's history of CSA. For example, it is possible that individuals who have been exposed to CSA may more frequently decline to participate in population surveys because they find the discussion of issues relating to sexual abuse to be painful, upsetting, or embarrassing. Conversely, those not exposed to sexual abuse may decline to participate on the grounds that, since they have not been sexually abused, they mistakenly believe that they have little to contribute (Haugaard & Emery, 1989).

In both cases, sources of sample loss are correlated with the individual's experiences of CSA and will lead to bias in prevalence estimates. In the first case, where a disproportionate number of those exposed to sexual abuse decline to participate, the study results will underestimate the true prevalence of abuse in the population, whereas in the second case, the true prevalence of abuse may be overestimated.

A more subtle source of sample selection bias may arise from the way in which the population from which the sample is drawn has been selected. In particular, many studies have examined rates of sexual abuse in selected communities or geographical areas, and it is possible that the social, cultural, and other characteristics of the community may influence the prevalence of abuse. Similarly, many studies have been restricted to female subjects, and this has resulted, until recently, in a relative neglect of the problem of sexual abuse in boys (Watkins & Bentovim, 1992). Although the choice of population definition will not threaten the validity of the prevalence estimate when it is applied to the population from which the sample is drawn, nonetheless, variations in population definitions and choice may lead to apparent differences in prevalence when the results of different studies are compared.

Sampling Variation

Variation in prevalence estimates will also arise from sampling variability. In all studies of the prevalence of sexual abuse, inferences about the true but nonobserved rate of abuse in the population being studied are made on the basis of inference from samples drawn from the population. However, sample estimates will not give an exact estimate of the true prevalence in the population, owing to the fact that prevalence estimates will vary with different samples. Unlike the other sources of variation in prevalence estimates, sampling variation can be assessed providing that the sample on which the prevalence estimate has been based is drawn at random. Estimates of the likely variation in the true prevalence of CSA in the population are given by the 95% confidence interval. This provides a range of values that 95 times out of 100 will contain the true population prevalence. The width of the confidence interval will be determined by the size of the sample and the prevalence of abuse within the sample. For example, with a sample of 200 participants having an observed prevalence of abuse of 20%, the 95% confidence interval ranges from 14.5% to 25.5%. The interpretation of this confidence interval is that 95 times out of 100 the interval will contain the true population prevalence.

To summarize, consideration of the issue of assessing the prevalence of sexual abuse in population samples suggests that there may be several reasons why these estimates have varied from study to study. These reasons include (a) variations in the definition of CSA, (b) variations in the methods by which abuse has been assessed, (c) variations in the characteristics of the samples being studied, and (d) variations reflecting random sampling errors.

RECENT POPULATION STUDIES OF THE PREVALENCE OF CSA

To illustrate the issues just raised, we present a review and analysis of the prevalence of sexual abuse as reported in recent general population studies of CSA. In selecting these studies, the following criteria were used.

First, studies were limited to those based on general population samples and to samples drawn from college students that had been published in the English language since 1990. Studies reporting prevalence estimates that were based on less than 100 subjects were excluded.

Tables 2.1 and 2.2 provide summaries of studies that reported on childhood sexual abuse within general population samples of females (Table 2.1) and males (Table 2.2). Each table identifies the study and describes the sample, the methods of assessment, the response rate obtained by the study, and the age used to define childhood. The studies in these tables can be divided into two groups: those studies that surveyed samples from the general population and those that surveyed samples of convenience, including college students and clinic attendees. Studies employing these different sampling frameworks are grouped separately in the tables. Estimates of the prevalence of CSA are

TABLE 2.1 Prevalence of Child Sexual Abuse (95% confidence intervals) Among Females for Studies Published Since 1990 and Based on Community Samples or Samples of Convenience

Study	Sample/Method of Data Collection	Definition of Childhood	Response Rate (%)	Any CSA	Contact CSA	Intercourse
Community Samples						
Anderson et al. (1993)	497 New Zealand women. Community sample. Face-to-face interview.	< 16 years	73.0	31.9 (27.8 to 36.0)	25.1 (21.3 to 28.9)	7.3 (5.0 to 9.6)
Bagley (1995)	898 Canadian women. National sample. Self-completed questionnaire.	< 17 years	85.8		17.6 (15.1 to 20.1)	
Bifulco et al. (1991)	286 British working-class women. Community sample. Face-to-face interview.	≤ 16 years	45.6		9.0 (5.7 to 12.3)	
Bushnell et al. (1992)	301 New Zealand women. Community sample. Face-to-face interview.	Not stated	60.9		13.0 (9.2 to 16.8)	
Elliot and Briere (1992)	2,963 United States women. National sample of professional women. Self-completed questionnaire.	< 16 years	55.0		26.9 (25.3 to 28.5)	
Fergusson et al. (1996)	516 New Zealand 18-year-olds. Community sample. Face-to-face interview.	< 16 years	80.6	17.3 (14.0 to 20.6)	13.0 (10.1 to 15.9)	5.6 (3.6 to 7.6)
Finkelhor et al. (1990)	1,481 United States adults. Random community sample. Telephone interview.	≤ 18 years	76.0	27.0 (24.7 to 29.3)		14.6 (12.8 to 16.4)

Finkelhor and Dziuba-Leatherman (1994)	958 United States 10- to 16-year-olds. Nationally representative community sample. Telephone interview.	≤ 10 to 16 years	72.2	15.3 (13.1 to 17.5)	6.9 (5.3 to 8.5)	1.3 (0.6 to 2.0)
Fleming (1997)	710 Australian voters. Community sample. Self-completed questionnaire.	≤ 16 years	65.0		20.3 (17.3 to 23.3)	5.4 (3.7 to 7.1)
Wonderlich et al. (1996)	1,099 United States women. Nationally representative sample. Self-completed questionnaire.	< 18 years	70.5	24.0 (21.5 to 26.5)		
Wyatt et al. (1992)	248 United States women. Face-to-face interview.	< 18 years	73	62.1 (56.1 to 68.1)	45.2 (39.0 to 51.4)	
Samples of Convenience						
Bendixen et al. (1994)	510 Norwegian university students. Self-completed questionnaire.	< 18 years	79.2	19.4 (16.0 to 22.8)		
Briere et al. (1994)	212 United States college students. Self-completed questionnaire.	≤ 16 years	100		21.7 (16.2 to 27.2)	
Fox and Gilbert (1994)	253 United States college students. Self-completed questionnaire.	< 17 years	Not stated		7.1 (3.9 to 10.3)	
Gould et al. (1994)	208 United States adults (18 years or older) attending family medicine practice. Self-completed questionnaire.	≤ 16 years	37.5		30.0 (23.8 to 36.2)	
Halperin et al. (1996)	568 Swiss 13- to 17-year-old children. School sample. Self-completed questionnaire.	≤ 13 to 17 years	93.5	33.8 (29.9 to 37.7)	20.4 (17.1 to 23.7)	5.6 (3.7 to 7.5)

(continued)

TABLE 2.1 (Continued)

Study	Sample/Method of Data Collection	Definition of Childhood	Response Rate (%)	Any CSA	Contact CSA	Intercourse
Hibbard et al. (1990)	2,041 United States 7th to 12th graders. School sample. Self-completed questionnaire.	≤ 13 to 18 years	69	12.9 (11.4 to 14.1)		
Hooper (1990)	418 British general practice attendees. Self-completed questionnaire.	Not stated	62	14.0 (10.7 to 17.3)	11.0 (8.0 to 14.0)	3.0 (1.4 to 4.6)
Kinzl et al. (1995)	202 Austrian university students. Self-completed questionnaire.	< 18 years	58	21.8 (16.1 to 27.5)		
Krugman et al. (1992)	224 Costa Rican students. University sample. Self-completed questionnaire.	Not stated	99.6	32.2 (26.1 to 38.3)		10.8 (6.8 to 14.8)
Lodico et al. (1996)	2,986 United States 9th- and 12th-grade students. School sample. Self-completed questionnaire.	≤ 15 to 18 years	95		16.5 (15.2 to 17.8)	
Nagy et al. (1994)	1,697 United States 8th- to 10th-grade students. School sample. Self-completed questionnaire.	≤ 13 to 17 years	87.5			12.6 (11.0 to 14.2)
Nagy et al. (1995)	3,124 United States 8th- to 10th-grade students. School sample. Self-completed questionnaire.	≤ 14 to 16 years	91.2		22.0 (20.5 to 23.5)	13.0 (11.8 to 14.2)

Study	Sample	Age	%	Estimate (95% CI)	Estimate (95% CI)
Nelson et al. (1994)	1,193 United States 9th to 12th graders. School sample. Self-completed questionnaire.	≤ 14 to 18 years	48.0	33.1 (30.4 to 35.8)	
Peters and Range (1995)	135 United States students. College sample. Self-completed questionnaire.	< 12 years	Not reported	31.9 (24.0 to 39.8)	19.3 (12.6 to 26.0)
Sariola and Uutela (1994)	3,769 students. 15- to 16-year-old Finnish high school students. Self-completed questionnaire.	< 16 years	85.2	8.0 (7.1 to 8.9)	
Springs and Friedrich (1992)	511 United States women. Community sample of clinic attendees. Self-completed questionnaire.	< 18 years	38.7		22.1 (18.5 to 25.7)
Wellman (1993)	657 United States students. College sample. Self-completed questionnaire.	Not stated	90.0	24.0 (20.7 to 27.3)	13.0 (10.4 to 15.6)
Zierler et al. (1991)	101 United States women. Face-to-face interview.	< 20 years	47.3		28.7 (19.9 to 37.5)

TABLE 2.2 Prevalence of Child Sexual Abuse (95% confidence intervals) Among Males for Studies Published Since 1990 and Based on Community Samples or Samples of Convenience

Study	Sample/Method of Data Collection	Definition of Childhood	Response Rate (%)	Any CSA	Contact CSA	Intercourse
Community Samples						
Bagley (1995)	935 Canadian men. National sample. Self-completed questionnaire.	<17 years	85.8		8.2 (6.4 to 10.0)	
Fergusson et al. (1996)	503 New Zealand 18-year-olds. Community sample. Face-to-face interview.	<16 years	80.6	3.4 (1.8 to 5.0)	3.0 (1.5 to 4.5)	1.4 (0.4 to 2.4)
Finkelhor et al. (1990)	1,145 United States adults. Random community sample. Telephone interview.	≤18 years	76.0	16.0 (13.9 to 18.1)		9.5 (7.8 to 11.2)
Finkelhor and Dziuba-Leatherman (1994)	1,042 United States 10- to 16-year-olds. Nationally representative community sample. Telephone interview.	≤10 to 16 years	72.2	5.9 (4.5 to 7.3)	1.0 (0.4 to 1.6)	0.0
Samples of Convenience						
Bendixen et al. (1994)	486 Norwegian university students. Self-completed questionnaire.	<18 years	71.7	3.5 (1.9 to 5.1)		
Briere et al. (1994)	106 United States college students. Self-completed questionnaire.	≤16 years	100.0		19.8 (12.2 to 27.4)	
Collings (1995)	284 United States college students. Self-completed questionnaire.	<18 years	87.0	29.0 (23.7 to 34.3)	9.0 (5.7 to 12.3)	
Gould et al. (1994)	84 United States adults (18 years or older) attending family medicine practice. Self-completed questionnaire.	≤16 years	37.5		12.0 (5.1 to 18.9)	

Study	Description	Age	%			
Halperin et al. (1996)	548 Swiss 13- to 17-year-old children. School sample. Self-completed questionnaire.	≤ 13 to 17 years	93.5	10.9 (8.3 to 13.5)	3.2 (1.7 to 4.7)	1.1 (0.2 to 2.0)
Hibbard et al. (1990)	1,957 United States 7th to 12th graders. School sample. Self-completed questionnaire.	Not stated	69.0	6.0 (2.7 to 9.3)		
Krugman et al (1992)	268 Costa Rican students. University sample. Self-completed questionnaire.	Not stated	99.6	12.8 (8.8 to 16.8)		6.4 (3.5 to 9.3)
Lodico et al. (1996)	3,238 United States 9th- and 12th-grade students. School sample. Self-completed questionnaire.	≤ 15 to 18 years	95		4.1 (3.4 to 4.8)	
Nagy et al. (1994)	1,321 United States 8th- to 10th-grade students. Self-completed questionnaire.	≤ 13 to 17 years	87.5			7.3 (5.9 to 8.7)
Nelson et al. (1994)	1,139 United States 9th to 12th graders. School sample. Self-completed questionnaire.	≤ 14 to 18 years	48.0	8.1 (6.5 to 9.7)		
Peters and Range (1995)	131 United States students. College sample. Self-completed questionnaire	< 12 years	Not reported	19.1 (12.4 to 25.8)	12.2 (6.6 to 17.8)	
Sariola and Uutela (1994)	3,666 Finnish 15- to 16-year-old high school students. Self-completed questionnaire.	< 16 years	85.2	3.0 (2.4 to 3.6)		
Wellman (1993)	167 United States students. College sample. Self-completed questionnaire.	Not stated	90.0	15.0 (9.6 to 20.4)	6.0 (2.4 to 9.6)	
Zierler et al. (1991)	85 United States men. Face-to-face interview.	< 20 years	47.3	15.0?		14.1 (6.7 to 21.5)

described using three criteria that range from a broad definition to a stringent definition. These definitions are

> Any CSA: This was based on a broad definition of CSA that classified children as being abused if any form of CSA, including noncontact CSA, was reported.
>
> Contact CSA: This definition restricted the estimate of the prevalence of CSA to only those episodes in which physical sexual contact occurred between the perpetrator and child or young person.
>
> Sexual Penetration: This was a stringent definition of CSA that required that the child or young person had been exposed to attempted or completed vaginal, oral, or anal penetration.

It should be noted that some of the estimates reported are not directly quoted in the original research and have been derived from secondary analysis of the published data.

Two features of the estimates shown in these tables are clearly evident. First, and predictably, the estimated prevalence of CSA varies with the stringency of the definition used. When we use definitions that include noncontact abuse, then 8% to 62.1% of females and 3% to 29% of males are classified as abused. On the other hand, by applying a stringent criterion requiring penetration or intercourse, we find that 1.3% to 28.7% of females and 1.1% to 14.1% of males are classified as abused. Estimates of the prevalence of abuse involving physical contact lie between these extremes.

Second, although there is a clear tendency for the prevalence of abuse to vary with the stringency of the definition of CSA, even within the same general definition of CSA, there is substantial variability in prevalence estimates. For example, using the criterion of any CSA, including noncontact abuse, prevalence estimates range from as low as 8% to as high as 62.1% for females, with the majority (80%) falling in the range of 15% to 33%. These results suggest that, although some of the variability in CSA estimates may be attributed to definitional variations, studies using the same or a similar definition of CSA produce widely varying estimates. This suggests the presence of study-specific features that, in turn, lead to between-study variations in prevalence estimates.

The studies reviewed vary in a number of ways that may have influenced estimates of prevalence. These include

- *Sample-related characteristics.* The studies reviewed have been based on samples drawn from different societies, communities, or population groups. It is possible that some of the apparent variation in prevalence rates may reflect genuine differences in rates of CSA in different cultures, communities, or population groups. The majority of studies report relatively high response rates, with most studies reporting response rates of 70% or better. This suggests that sample selection biases due to nonparticipation in research are unlikely to have had a major effect on estimates.

It is important to note that some of the previously mentioned studies have relied on surveys of high school or college students (Briere et al., 1994; Collings, 1995; Halperin et al., 1996; Hibbard et al., 1990; Krugman, Mata, & Krugman, 1992; Nagy, Adcock, & Nagy, 1994; Nagy, DiClemente, & Adcock, 1995; Peters & Range, 1995; Sariola & Uutela, 1994; Wellman, 1993). However, this procedure may produce unsatisfactory samples, as it excludes from study those individuals who do not attend school or university and also those students who, for whatever reason, are absent from school on the day of the data collection. In addition, it has been suggested that rates of exposure to CSA may be lower among college students than among the general population (Peters et al., 1986). Thus, these exclusions may to lead to an underestimation of the prevalence of CSA within the general population.

- *Measurement-related factors.* The studies described have used a range of approaches and methodologies to assess the prevalence of abuse. First, studies have varied in the extent of their questions, with some methods for assessing CSA being based on approaches that asked a single general question about CSA (Hibbard et al., 1990; Wellman, 1993) and others based on multiple items or methods of assessment (Anderson et al., 1993; Fergusson et al., 1996). It could be suggested that, in part, variations in the prevalence of CSA reflect variations in the extent and intensity of questioning about childhood sexual experiences (Peters et al., 1986). Here, it is notable that the studies using a single question to define abuse (Hibbard et al., 1990; Wellman, 1993), as a general rule, reported lower rates of CSA than studies based on multiple questions and items.

  A second dimension on which studies varied concerned the method by which CSA questions were administered. In some studies, methods of face-to-face interviewing were used (Anderson et al., 1993; Bifulco, Brown, & Adler, 1991; Bushnell, Wells, & Oakley-Browne, 1992; Fergusson et al., 1996; Wonderlich, Wilsnack, Wilsnack, & Harris, 1996), whereas in other studies data were collected by self-report questionnaires (Briere et al., 1994; Collings, 1995; Halperin et al., 1996; Hibbard et al., 1990; Krugman et al., 1992; Nagy et al., 1994, 1995; Peters & Range, 1995; Sariola & Uutela, 1994; Springs & Friedrich, 1992; Wellman, 1993) or telephone interview (Finkelhor et al., 1990; Finkelhor & Dziuba-Leatherman, 1994). There is, however, no clear trend to suggest that studies using telephone or self-report methods produce consistently higher or lower rates of CSA than methods based on face-to-face interviews.

- *The definition of childhood.* Studies have also varied in their definition of childhood. Although a number of studies have used an upper limit of age 16 to define childhood (Anderson et al., 1993; Bifulco et al., 1991; Briere et al., 1994; Fergusson et al., 1996), others have used age limits as low as 12 years (Peters & Range, 1995), have studied sexual abuse in samples varying in age (Finkelhor & Dziuba-Leatherman, 1994; Halperin et al., 1996; Hibbard et al., 1990; Nagy et al., 1994, 1995), or have used an upper limit of age 18 (Finkelhor et al., 1990; Springs & Friedrich, 1992; Wonderlich et al., 1996). In turn, these variations in the age range used to define child sexual abuse may influence prevalence estimates, but there is no clear trend for studies using younger or older individuals in their samples to show consistently higher or lower prevalence rates.

- *Sampling error.* All estimates in the table quote 95% confidence intervals, and, as may be seen, in a majority of cases these limits are relatively narrow, reflecting the large sample size. Inspection of the confidence-interval estimates suggests that a negligible amount of between-study variation is likely to arise from sampling variation.

More generally, the results suggest considerable unexplained variation in estimates of the prevalence of abuse. Nonetheless, even given this variability in estimates, a number of conclusions may be drawn with some degree of confidence. Specifically, the estimates based on reports of any CSA clearly suggest that exposure to some form of unwanted sexual attention during childhood is all too common. Estimates for females suggest that up to one third of women may report such exposure, with the majority of studies suggesting prevalence somewhere in the interval between 15% and 30%. Similar estimates for males suggest that up to 30% of males may report sexual abuse of some form, with most estimates lying within the interval from 3% to 15%. Of perhaps greater concern is the number of children who report being exposed to acts of sexual abuse that involve sexual penetration. The estimates suggest that up to 13% of females and 11.3% of males may report abuse of this severity, with the majority of studies reporting prevalence figures in the range of 5% to 10%.

It is important to place the prevalence figures for severe abuse involving sexual penetration in context. There is often a tendency to treat percentages below 10% as reflecting uncommon or rare events, but even low prevalence rates may lead to large numbers of children who are exposed to risk. For example, if the true prevalence of severe, physically intrusive childhood sexual abuse was as low as 3%, this would still imply that every school class of 30 children would contain one child who was the victim of such severe abuse. Looked at from this perspective, the figures on the prevalence of more severe forms of abuse involving penetration clearly suggest that childhood sexual abuse cannot be regarded as an inconsequential problem of childhood.

This is irrespective of debates about the true prevalence of abuse when less stringent definitions are applied. The variability in prevalence estimates has important implications for the ways in which CSA is reported and discussed. It is not uncommon in debates to encounter strong claims that some substantial fraction (usually a quarter or a third) of the child population is subject to sexual abuse (Peters et al., 1986). Such claims are potentially misleading in two ways—the large variability in estimates of the prevalence of CSA probably precludes making statements with this degree of precision, and, as a general rule, it would seem preferable to quote a range of estimates rather than rely on a single estimate. More important, in the minds of the public and many policymakers, the term sexual abuse is implicitly equated with the more severely intrusive incidents of child rape and molestation. The reality is that the majority of those cases meeting general criteria for CSA are not, in fact, the grosser forms of abuse. Propagating high prevalence figures for child sexual abuse without making it clear that this covers a wide range of unwanted sexual experiences risks causing these claims to be regarded as implausible, and it encourages distrust of the findings and the researchers (Peters et al., 1986).

PROPOSALS TO IMPROVE THE MEASUREMENT, CLASSIFICATION, AND REPORTING OF CSA

There have often been strong and emotive public debates about the prevalence of CSA, with some arguing that CSA is an epidemic that afflicts a large number of children (Herman, 1981; Saphira, 1985) and others expressing doubts about this evidence (Rich, 1990). The data in the published literature on CSA have done relatively little to resolve such debates because, by selectively quoting the evidence and by heightening or leveling issues about the extent of abuse, it becomes possible to support almost any position concerning the prevalence of abuse. If substantial progress is to be made, a methodological evaluation of this area is needed.

Classification of the Spectrum of Child Abuse

The experience of sexual abuse in childhood can vary from relatively nonintrusive episodes of noncontact abuse to severe and brutal sexual violation. This lumping together of widely disparate events has, as already noted, been unhelpful. We need to develop taxonomies and classifications that describe the nature and extent of abusive acts. Some work in this direction has already begun, with a number of studies using general measures of abuse severity that are based on the type of abusive experience reported (e.g.,

Anderson et al., 1993; Fergusson et al., 1996; Finkelhor & Dziuba-Leatherman, 1994; Halperin et al., 1996). There is, however, a need to extend such methods of classification to take into account multiple criteria, including the duration of the abuse, the victim's relationship to the abuser, the form of coercion employed, the victim's perceptions of the abuse incident, and at what age the abuse was perpetrated.

Improvement and Investigation of Research Methodologies

A substantial amount of the variation in prevalence estimates among studies of CSA may arise from differences in research methodologies. However, of all the complex issues that arise in the measurement of CSA, issues relating to choice of methodology and its impact on rates of CSA are perhaps the easiest to address. In principle, it is possible to design randomized field trials to look at the extent to which the reported prevalence of CSA varies with different approaches. More generally, these procedures may be modeled on the large number of studies in the survey research literature that have used experimental or quasi-experimental methods to examine the extent to which findings and conclusions are sensitive to the methods by which data are collected (see Schwarz & Sudman, 1992).

Assessment of the Reliability and Validity of Abuse Reports

The reliability of a measure broadly reflects the extent to which that measure is repeatable and consistent, whereas the validity of a measure reflects the extent to which the measure provides an accurate account of what it purports to measure. Although relatively little is known about the reliability of CSA reports, the assessment of reporting reliability is fairly straightforward, through the use of test/retest methods in which the same sample of individuals are questioned on two or more occasions to determine the consistency with which abuse experiences are reported. Evidence of high consistency of reports over measurement periods would suggest good reliability, whereas inconsistencies may suggest unreliability. There appear to have been few studies of the reliability of CSA reporting, which reflects that most research in this area has been based upon cross-sectional research rather than longitudinal or panel studies. Nonetheless, these issues have been examined by Martin et al. (1993) in a study of a sample of New Zealand women. These authors found moderate-to-good stability in the reporting of CSA episodes by a sample of New Zealand women who were studied on two occasions.

The assessment of the validity of CSA reporting poses profound difficulties. The assessment of CSA is almost invariably based on the retrospective reporting of the memories of events that cannot usually be confirmed by appeal to external sources of information. Thus, there is no gold standard against which the accuracy of this reporting may be judged. There are, however, a number of approaches that may provide some background and insight into the validity of CSA reporting. These include

- *Comparison of subject reports with other sources of data.* In certain cases it may be possible to compare the individual's account of CSA experiences with agency or official record data of sexual abuse to examine the extent to which those known to have experienced sexual abuse have accurately recalled or disclosed these experiences. This methodology was, for example, used in a recent study by Williams (1994), who compared the retrospective reports of a group of women known to have been subject to abuse in childhood. This study revealed that a substantial proportion (38%) of those known to be abused either couldn't recall or wouldn't disclose the specific abuse incidents, although only 12% of those who were known to have been abused did not report some incident of CSA, even if it was not the one listed in the records that were available to the researchers. More generally, in some research designs it may be possible to compare the respondent's reports of childhood sexual abuse with the accounts of a "significant other," or confidante, who knows the respondent well. Although these methodologies fall far short of providing a gold standard by which the accuracy of CSA reporting can be judged, they may give insights into the extent to which respondent's reports of CSA differ from accounts provided by other sources. The difficulty with such approaches is that given the known low levels of reporting abuse at the time it occurs, as was already discussed, such confirmatory efforts can only give support in the minority of cases where there occurred contemporaneous disclosure. Investigations of this type must be conducted with care to ensure that the respondents are fully aware of, and agreeable to, their reports being compared with those provided by alternative sources.
- *Analysis of changes in reporting.* In longitudinal or panel designs, it may be possible to examine the factors associated with those who give changing reports of abuse to determine the extent to which abuse disclosure may be dependent on other factors, including the respondents' mental state at the time of the interview and other related variables (Bifulco et al., 1991).

Although none of these methods offer foolproof or watertight methods for validating CSA reports, they may clarify some aspects of reporting behavior and the more general context within which CSA reports are made. It is also clear that despite such methodological refinements, issues relating to the validity of CSA reports are likely to remain a major consideration in both the interpretation of prevalence estimates and the analysis of the causes and consequences of CSA, to say nothing of their evidentiary weight in court cases involving prosecutions or compensation claims. We will revisit the issue of the accuracy of reporting and testimony in the final chapter.

CONCLUDING COMMENT

At the beginning of this chapter, we asked what appeared to be a relatively simple question: What percentage of children are exposed to sexual abuse? The reader may be forgiven for feeling that we have not answered this question but, rather, have turned what seemed to be a simple question into a vast and complex problem. This, in fact, has been our intention. In particular, the popular rendition of the literature on CSA has frequently resulted in trite conclusions that are chanted like sacred mantras about the proportion of children who are sexually abused. However, underlying these trite and perhaps socially convenient claims, there is a complex body of evidence that is both highly variable and by no means easy to interpret. Reducing this evidence to claims that one in four (or whatever fraction of) children is subject to sexual abuse conceals the very real uncertainties, debates, and issues that surround this evidence. What we have sought to do in this chapter is to draw the reader's attention to the large variation in prevalence estimates, the likely factors contributing to this variation, and the need for care and caution in presenting and interpreting this evidence.

Considerable uncertainty remains regarding the evidence about the prevalence of abuse, but, nevertheless, a number of things are clear. First and foremost, exposure to unwanted sexual attention in childhood is not uncommon and, more important, there is consistent evidence to suggest that 5% to 10% of children are exposed to severely abusive acts involving actual or attempted sexual penetration. Second, the results show that sexual abuse is by no means confined to females. Whereas, typically, prevalence estimates suggest a higher rate of all types of sexual abuse among females, there are, nonetheless, not insubstantial numbers of males who are also exposed; and when it comes to the severe forms of abuse involving sexual penetration, the estimates do not greatly differ for boys and girls.

Beyond these specific issues, our analysis suggests the need for a reevaluation of the methodologies applied in this area of research. Studies over the past 20 years have sought both to document sexual abuse in our communities and to provide the epidemiological underpinnings for the development of programs and services for abused children. One of the consequences of this entirely laudable aim has been to produce a large body of very uneven and very difficult-to-interpret literature. The time has come to move beyond studies that show that sexual abuse is an important childhood problem and to address the fundamental issues relating to the definition, classification, measurement, and interpretation of abuse statistics. In this respect, there is a clear need for methodological advances to develop more refined classifications of abuse; to assess the extent to which different methodologies may influence the estimate of the prevalence of abuse; to examine the stability and reliability of abuse reports; and to address, as far as possible, issues relating to the validity and accuracy of abuse reporting.

3

VICTIMS AND PERPETRATORS

This chapter presents a review of two closely related issues. First, we will examine the factors that are associated with children who are at high risk of exposure to sexual abuse and consider the extent to which it may be possible to identify at risk children from a knowledge of their family as well as of social and related factors. Second, we will present an overview of what is currently known of the characteristics of those individuals who sexually molest children.

CHARACTERISTICS OF ABUSED CHILDREN

Gender and CSA

The focus in writing and research on CSA has tended to be on female victims (Finkelhor & Baron, 1986). This gender bias in the literature has obscured issues relating to the sexual abuse of male children (Collings, 1995; Dhaliwal, Gauzas, Antonowicz, & Ross, 1996; Watkins & Bentovim, 1992). Although CSA is more common among females, a sizable minority of those exposed to CSA are male. In a review of the literature up to 1986, Finkelhor and Baron (1986) estimated that rates of CSA were 2.5 times higher in females than in males.

Examination of the prevalence studies reviewed in Tables 2.1 and 2.2 shows that studies have reported female:male sex ratios that have ranged from as low as 1.1 to as high as 6.4 with the majority of studies reporting sex ratios in the region of 1.5 to 4.0. Table 3.1 presents a re-analysis of the evidence reviewed in Tables 2.1 and 2.2. This table reports weighted average estimates of the prevalence of CSA in males and females and the corresponding female:male sex ratios implied by these estimates. The table shows that, depending on the definition of CSA, sex ratios range from 1.8 to 3.4. Further inspection of the table shows that for severe abuse involving sexual

TABLE 3.1 Weighted Average Rates of Any CSA, Contact CSA, and Intercourse for Females and Males From Studies Reported in Tables 2.1
and 2.2

	Females	Males	
Extent of Abuse	%	%	Female:Male Ratio
Any CSA	19.1	7.2	2.7
Contact CSA	19.2	5.7	3.4
Intercourse	10.1	5.7	1.8

penetration, the sex ratio is smaller than for other definitions. This reflects the fact that gender differences in rates of severe CSA are not as marked as differences for other forms of CSA. The weight of the evidence clearly favors the view that females are at greater risk of CSA, with this risk being in the region of two to three times higher than the risk for males.

Age of Onset of Abuse

The ascertainment of the age of onset of CSA has often been based on retrospective reports of abuse incidents, with these reports being made many years later. Thus, it is likely that incidents of abuse occurring during the preschool years may be underreported. Finkelhor and Baron (1986), reviewing the literature available at that time, reported a median age of onset of abuse between 10 and 11 years. The studies of Anderson et al. (1993) indicated a sharp rise in the frequency of the first incident of abuse between 4 and 8 years of age, with reports of CSA peaking at age 11 and with the vast majority of the females being abused prior to the onset of menstruation. The age of onset of CSA has been reported to be significantly lower for girls (Baker & Duncan, 1985). CSA is most likely to occur in prepubertal or peripubertal children rather than in sexually mature young girls. The victims are usually unequivocally children, not young women.

These trends are illustrated in Figure 3.1, which shows the relationship between age and risk of CSA derived from the series of studies reviewed by Finkelhor and Baron (1986). This figure shows generally increasing rates of CSA up to the age of 11 years, with rates stabilizing thereafter to a rate of 1.5% to 4% per annum, with the peak ages of risk of CSA occurring being between 10 and 12 years. It is possible, however, that much of the apparent difference in CSA risk between the preschool years and adolescence arises

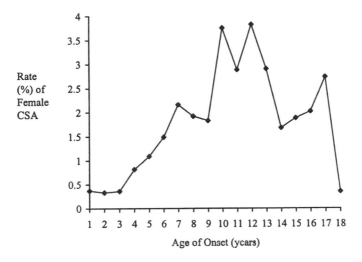

Figure 3.1. Rate of CSA, by Age of Onset

because rates of CSA in young children may be underreported relative to the reporting of episodes of CSA following middle childhood.

The Characteristics of Children Exposed to CSA

A growing number of studies have examined the social and family characteristics of children exposed to CSA in an attempt to develop profiles of the social circumstances associated with elevated risks of CSA. The following trends have emerged from these studies:

- *Social class and CSA.* In many areas of child abuse research, clear linkages have been found between measures of social class, social stratification, or social disadvantage and abuse risks, with children from socially disadvantaged families emerging as being at higher risk of physical and emotional abuse (Connelly & Straus, 1992; Dubowitz, Hampton, Bithoney, & Newberger, 1987; Martin & Walters, 1982; Whipple & Webster-Stratton, 1991). CSA appears to be an exception to this trend for child abuse to be related to social class. A growing number of studies have reported a weak or no association between measures of family socioeconomic status and risks of CSA (Bergner, Delgado, & Graybill, 1994; Fergusson et al., 1996; Fleming, Mullen, & Bammer, 1997; Finkelhor, 1993; Mullen et al., 1996). This finding suggests that risks of CSA are largely unrelated to social class and that children from different social strata may be exposed to generally similar risks of CSA.

• *Family functioning and CSA*. Although risks of CSA appear to have little relationship to patterns of socioeconomic disadvantage, there has been a growing body of evidence linking CSA to a series of measures of family function and dysfunction. These findings have included

1. Linkages between CSA and measures of marital dysfunction, including parental divorce/separation and marital conflict (Fergusson et al., 1996; Fleming et al., 1997; Mullen et al., 1993; Stern, Lynch, Oates, O'Toole, & Cooney, 1995).

2. Linkages between CSA and patterns of family change and particularly the presence of stepparents in the family (Fergusson et al., 1996; Mullen et al., 1993; Fleming et al., 1997; Paradise, Rose, Sleeper, & Nathanson, 1994; Russell, 1986).

3. Linkages between CSA and parental adjustment and particularly parental alcoholism and criminality (Brown & Anderson, 1991; Fergusson et al., 1996; Mullen et al., 1993; Paradise et al., 1994; Stern et al., 1995).

4. Linkages between CSA and measures of parent/child attachment (Fergusson et al., 1996; Fleming et al., 1997; Mullen et al., 1993).

The family profile of the child most at risk of CSA that emerges from these analyses is that of a child reared in a home that is characterized by multiple signs of difficulty and dysfunction spanning: marital conflict and disharmony, family change, stepparenthood, parental adjustment problems, and impaired parent-child attachments. There are two possible explanations for these pervasive linkages between risks of CSA and family functioning. The first is that the family factors associated with CSA may, in fact, be markers for families likely to contain a CSA perpetrator. Given that most perpetrators are not immediate family members, it is more likely that the linkages reflect family environments that, in various ways, may expose children to risks of CSA as a result of limited parental care, supervision, and protection of children.

This issue has recently been examined in a study by Fergusson and colleagues (1996), who compared the family backgrounds of children who were exposed to intrafamilial CSA with children who were exposed to extrafamilial CSA. This analysis found that children exposed to intrafamilial and extrafamilial abuse came from similar backgrounds. This result supports the view that measures of family functioning are linked to risks of CSA by generalized processes in which family dysfunction creates a social and family ecology that places children at risk of both extrafamilial and intrafamilial abuse.

CSA and Other Forms of Child Abuse

A finding that has emerged from an increasing number of studies is that children who are exposed to CSA have also been physically and emotionally abused (Fergusson et al., 1997; Finkelhor & Dzuiba-Leatherman, 1994; Fleming et al., 1997; Hibbard et al., 1990; Mullen et al., 1996). Mullen et al. (1996) found that women with histories of CSA had rates of childhood physical abuse that were 5.3 times higher and rates of emotional abuse that were 3.0 times higher than women who did not report a history of CSA.

There are at least two reasons for apparent comorbidities of child abuse. First, these comorbidities may reflect the fact that the family environments that encourage CSA are also linked to other forms of child abuse. There is broad support for this view in the literature on child abuse, to the extent that there are clear overlaps between the family factors associated with different types of child abuse. The second possible explanation is that the apparent comorbidity may reflect a data collection artifact that arises because individuals who are prepared to disclose one type of abuse may also be more willing to disclose other types of abuse.

The Individual Characteristics of Children at Risk of CSA

An area of research that merits attention is the extent to which children have characteristics that may increase their risks of being exposed to CSA. Characteristics of potential interest include physical attractiveness, height, weight, temperamental characteristics, and intelligence.

Although Finkelhor and Baron (1986) propose the need to study the individual characteristics of CSA victims that may increase their vulnerability to abuse, there appears to be relatively little research in this area. Elliott, Browne, and Kilcoyne (1995) have reported on a study of 91 men convicted of CSA offenses, in which CSA perpetrators described the strategies by which they selected and enlisted CSA victims. They identified factors such as whether the child was pretty, the way the child was dressed, and whether the child was young or small or innocent and trusting. While these findings are tentative and limited by the sampling of known offenders, they are nonetheless consistent with the view that certain child characteristics may be more attractive to CSA perpetrators and may place children with these characteristics at greater risk.

In a recent study, Fergusson and colleagues (1997) examined the relationship between the age of menarche and rates of sexual abuse in a sample of 520 females. This analysis showed the presence of a small but marginally significant tendency for girls with early menarche (< 13 years) to report higher rates of CSA. This result may suggest that early sexual maturation may be a factor that somehow increases risks of CSA. This conclusion is theoretically defensible to the extent that children who show early sexual maturation may be more attractive to some CSA perpetrators but may lack the social skills and sophistication to recognize the early signs of sexual advances by CSA perpetrators. Mullen and colleagues (1996) failed to find associations to childhood factors such as being a follower and lacking friends, but they did note a weak link to childhood shyness.

CAN CHILDREN AT RISK OF CSA BE IDENTIFIED?

From the previous account, one can see that it is possible to construct a social profile of the child who is most likely to be sexually abused. This child is likely to be female, to be between 8 and 12 years of age, to be reared in a family situation characterized by a range of dysfunctional features, and possibly to be also subjected to other forms of child abuse. The development of this profile naturally leads to the thought that information on family characteristics may be used to predict or identify children at risk of CSA. If this were possible, the development of predictive indices could play a valuable role in both the prevention and diagnosis of CSA. The prospects of using family and social characteristics to identify children at risk of CSA have been discussed by a number of authors (Bergner et al., 1994; Fergusson et al., 1996; Finkelhor, 1993), all of whom have concluded that the identification of children at risk of CSA is likely to be highly imprecise and potentially misleading.

The reasons for this can be seen from a recent study reported by Fergusson and colleagues (1996), who examined the extent to which it was possible to identify CSA using prospectively collected measures of family and social circumstances. Although this study identified a number of individual and family predictors of CSA that included gender, marital conflict, parental attachment, parental bonding, and parental problems, it was also evident that the extent to which it was possible to predict CSA on the basis of these characteristics was very limited. In their analysis, Fergusson et al. (1996) were able to identify groups of children who had as low as a 1.8% risk of CSA to as high a risk as 25.8%. They point out that, whereas discrimination of risks of CSA on the basis of family data was possible, even among the highest-risk group the majority of children were not, in fact, sexually abused.

It is clear that the application of such findings to the identification of families in which CSA is likely would produce adverse effects in which families may be falsely labeled as having the potential to be prone to CSA when, in fact, the majority of children identified as living in high-risk situations may not be subject to abuse.

METHODOLOGICAL ISSUES IN THE STUDY OF THE SOCIAL BACKGROUND OF CHILDREN EXPOSED TO CSA

Although there is an emerging body of evidence that has identified a relatively consistent set of risk factors associated with CSA, as with all areas of CSA research this evidence is compromised by a series of threats to validity that make interpretation complex. These threats to validity include:

- *Recall bias.* Of necessity, many accounts of the family circumstances associated with CSA have been based on studies of adult populations, in which those disclosing CSA have provided retrospective accounts of their childhood. A liability of such accounts is that the individuals' exposure to CSA may color their accounts of childhood in ways that emphasize adverse childhood events and circumstances. In addition, those who are willing to disclose CSA may also have a greater willingness to disclose adversities during their childhood. The possibility of these types of reporting and recall biases occurring may mean that, in part, the apparent linkages between family factors and CSA could reflect biases in reporting rather than genuine associations between family context and CSA risks.

- *Difficulties in determining causal precedence.* A related issue that arises from the retrospective reporting of events that occurred in childhood is that of determining the temporal and causal sequencing of family circumstances and CSA exposures. In particular, it may be argued that a number of the risk factors that are associated with CSA may, in fact, reflect the consequences of CSA for family functioning rather than the effects of family functioning on the risks of CSA. For example, it may be suggested that linkages between CSA and such factors as marital conflict and poor parent/child attachments arise not because these factors increase risks of CSA but, rather, because the presence of CSA may lead to both marital conflict and impaired parent/child attachments. Clearly, to examine this issue requires studies that make it possible to ascertain the timing of both abuse onset and key family events and circumstances.

- *Sample selection bias.* A number of studies that have examined the differences in the backgrounds of children exposed and not exposed to CSA have employed research designs in which the backgrounds of children known to be exposed to sexual abuse have been contrasted with the backgrounds of a control series of nonabused children (Paradise et al., 1994; Stern et al., 1995). These studies are subject to potentially serious sample selection biases that could lead to a misleading impression of linkages between family background and CSA risks. In particular, children who are known to have been sexually abused comprise a selected and nonrandom group of all children who have been exposed to abuse. It is easy to imagine that the processes by which these children come to attention may be influenced by other family characteristics, including marital conflict, parental adjustment difficulties, and related factors. The net result is that studies based on children known to be sexually abused may be biased toward the overinclusion of children who have been both sexually abused and exposed to family dysfunction. In turn, this may lead to biased or misleading estimates of the linkages between CSA and family factors.

The best means of addressing many of these issues of recall bias, causal priority, and sample selection would clearly be through a prospective study in which a large and representative sample of children was studied from birth into young adulthood, with regular assessments of both family circumstances and the onset of CSA being collected. This design would make it possible to examine the extent to which the onset of CSA was associated with family and social factors that preceded this onset. However, there are certain almost insuperable practical difficulties in implementing such a design, which center around the difficulties of obtaining measures of CSA onset in a general child population. These difficulties are likely to be of two types. First, to collect such data would probably require that parents, teachers, and children be enlisted as informants to describe the child's exposure to CSA at each point of study. It is likely that such research would encounter considerable resistance from these informants. Second, and equally important, a prospective study of CSA poses complex ethical difficulties in the responses of researchers to CSA exposures. Ethically, evidence that children are subject to CSA would require research staff to intervene to refer children to sources of support and assistance. However, the knowledge that CSA disclosure would be followed by this response may have the effect of inhibiting informants from disclosing CSA. It is also likely that researchers would face complex legal problems in situations in which disclosures of CSA proved to be false or unfounded. For all of these reasons, a fully prospective study of CSA in childhood poses practical and ethical problems that are likely to prevent such research (Bertolli et al., 1995).

A weaker design that preserves some of the features of the fully prospective study but that avoids many of the difficulties just outlined is to embed research on CSA into the context of large prospective studies. A research design that appears both ethically defensible and feasible would involve the study of a large and representative cohort of children from birth to adulthood, during which information on childhood social and family circumstances was collected at regular intervals. At the point that cohort members became adults, it would then be possible to obtain retrospective reports of CSA in a way that would avoid the practical and ethical difficulties that are associated with the prospective collection of CSA data. To date, only one study has used this approach. In particular, Fergusson et al. (1996) have reported the results of an 18-year longitudinal study that examined the linkages between prospectively measured childhood and family circumstances and retrospective reports of CSA. The trends that emerged from this semiprospective design produced results that were clearly convergent with fully retrospective studies and with studies that have compared children known to be sexually abused with control children. This convergence of evidence from a triangulation of three different research designs (retrospective studies, clinic-based studies, and partial prospective designs) tends to suggest that although a theoretical case can be made to suggest that linkages between CSA and family or childhood conditions may reflect sampling and recall biases the trends in the evidence suggest that these linkages are likely to be nonartifactual and to reflect that children exposed to CSA tend to come from family backgrounds that show evidence of pervasive signs of dysfunction and difficulty. However, much remains to be learned about the causal sequencing of family dysfunction and the onset of CSA, and there is a clear need for further semiprospective studies that replicate and extend the existing work in this area.

CHARACTERISTICS OF CHILD MOLESTERS

There have been two research designs used to examine the characteristics of CSA perpetrators. First, a number of studies have relied on reports of CSA victims about the characteristics of the abuse perpetrator. These studies have the advantage that they can show the characteristics of abuse perpetrators in unselected (nonclinic) populations, but they have the liability that information provided by CSA victims is limited to relatively superficial characteristics of the perpetrator, which may include age, gender, and relationship to the victim. Other studies have developed a more detailed profile of CSA perpetrators by studying the characteristics of individuals known to be child molesters. Typically, samples have been drawn from groups of individuals

under treatment, supervision, or care because of their past history of perpe-
trating CSA. Studies using this design have the advantage that it is possible
to develop an in-depth profile of child molesters. However, a limitation of
the approach is that child molesters who come to official attention may not
be a representative sample of CSA perpetrators. Nonetheless, even allowing
for the limitations of this literature, it becomes possible to develop a preliminary account of child molesters.

The Age Distribution of Offenders. All studies to date have reported wide
variation in the age of molesters, ranging from those who are the same age
or even younger than their victims to those who are over 60 years old. The
only clear conclusion of this research is that CSA is not confined to any
particular age group, although many studies suggest that the majority of
perpetrators are in the age range of 15 to 45 years, with peak levels in the
18- to 25-year age group.

Gender and CSA. Until recently, it was believed that nearly all CSA perpetrators were male (Araji & Finkelhor, 1986). However, recent studies
that have examined CSA in males have revealed that a minority of perpetrators are, in fact, female (Bagley, 1995; Fergusson et al., 1996; Finkelhor
et al., 1990; Halperin et al., 1996; Kinzl, Traweger, & Biefl, 1995; Krugman
et al., 1992). The trends in current evidence on the gender of CSA perpetrators is summarized in Table 3.2, which shows estimates of the proportion of male perpetrators reported by the studies described in Tables 2.1
and 2.2. Separate figures are reported for female, male, and total population samples. There is evidence of clear differences in the rate of male perpetration, depending on the gender of the CSA victims. For female victims,
it is clear that almost all perpetrators are male, with estimates of the percentage of male perpetrators ranging from 92.0% to 99.2%, with the
weighted average rate of male perpetration being 97.5%. However, for
males a somewhat different picture emerges, with study estimates suggesting that between 63.2% and 85.7% of perpetrators are male, with the
weighted average estimate showing an estimate of 78.7% male perpetration
(and by implication, a 21.3% perpetration rate for females). Estimates
based on total samples including males and females show rates of male
perpetration that fall between the rates for female and male victims, with
the weighted average giving a male perpetration rate of 92.5%.

TABLE 3.2 Rates of Male Perpetrators for Males and Females Who Have Experienced CSA, From Studies Reporting Gender of Perpetrator

Study	% Male Perpetrators		
	Female Victims	Male Victims	Total
Anderson et al. (1993)	98.0	—	—
Bagley (1995)	98.7	76.8	91.9
Bendixen et al. (1994)	99.2	85.7	97.1
Fergusson et al. (1996)	99.1	65.0	93.9
Finkelhor et al. (1990)	98.1	82.8	93.7
Halperin et al. (1996)	93.6	79.6	90.5
Kinzl et al. (1995)	97.7	—	—
Krugman et al. (1992)	92.0	63.2	80.7
Overall	97.5	78.7	92.5

Finally, although present evidence suggests that there is a minority of female CSA perpetrators, it has also been argued that rates of CSA perpetration by females are likely to be underreported as a result of a lack of recognition of CSA by female perpetrators (Peluso & Putnam, 1996).

The Relationship Between CSA Perpetrators and Victims. It is frequently assumed that the majority of CSA incidents involve various forms of incest in which family members engage in sexual behavior with children within the family. Research indicates that this stereotype of sexual abuse as incest is inaccurate and that the majority of child molesters are not members of the victim's immediate family. This issue is examined in Table 3.3, which summarizes findings from a series of studies reported in Tables 2.1 and 2.2 that have provided accounts of the relationship between victim and perpetrator. This table shows the percentages of CSA perpetrators who were (a) natural parents; (b) stepparents; (c) siblings; (d) other relatives not within the immediate family; (e) acquaintances, including, for example, friends, neighbors, boyfriends, and girlfriends; and (f) strangers who were not known to the CSA victim prior to the incident.

TABLE 3.3 Relationship of Perpetrator to the Child, From Studies Reporting This Relationship

Study	Percentage of Perpetrators Who Were:					
	Natural Parent	Stepparent	Sibling	Other Relative	Acquaintance	Stranger
Anderson et al. (1993)	5.0	2.0	9.0	22.3	46.3	15.0
Bagley (1995)		18.3		15.7	47.2	18.7
Bifulco et al. (1991)	16.0	12.0	4.0	24.0	20.0	24.0
Fergusson et al. (1996)	1.5	5.3	6.8	9.8	47.7	28.8
Finkelhor et al. (1990)	2.1	2.1	1.7	17.7	49.7	26.7
Kinzl et al. (1995)		20.5		18.2	31.8	29.5
Krugman et al. (1992)	3.3	3.9	26.1		45.1	21.6
Wellman (1993)	12.0	3.3	31.7		37.2	15.8
Overall [1]	3.3	2.7	4.5	18.3	47.8	23.4

[1] Overall percentages of weighted mean based only on those studies that reported rates for all categories of perpetrator.

The following conclusions may be drawn from the table:

1. Between 5.9% and 32.0% of CSA incidents were committed by family members, including parents, stepparents, and siblings. The weighted average estimate from this series of studies suggests that, overall, 10.4% of CSA incidents involved close family members.

2. In nearly all studies, the most frequently reported perpetrators were acquaintances of the victim. These individuals span a wide range of people, including family, friends, and neighbors. The studies reviewed suggest that in the region of 20% to 50% of CSA perpetrators are described in this category, with the weighted average estimate suggesting that, overall, 47.8% of CSA perpetrators were described as acquaintances.

3. CSA perpetrated by parent figures is relatively uncommon. Estimates of the proportion of CSA incidents committed by natural parents range from as low as 1.5% to as high as 16%, with the weighted average estimate suggesting that 3.3% of CSA incidents were perpetrated by natural fathers. Estimates for the rate of perpetration by stepparents show a similar range of values to rates of perpetration by natural parents, with the weighted average suggesting that 2.7% of all CSA incidents studied were committed by stepparents. However, the fact that rates of perpetration by stepparents are similar to rates of perpetration by natural parents suggests that stepparents are more likely to commit CSA episodes since there are far fewer stepparents in the population than natural parents. Anderson and colleagues (1993) estimated that stepparents had risks of committing CSA that were in the region of 10 times higher than those of natural parents. The higher rates of CSA perpetration among stepparents has been attributed to a number of factors that include the possibility that the taboos against stepparent-stepchild contact are less stringent or that the parent-child bonding that occurs during the child's infancy may inhibit sexual contact (Finkelhor & Baron, 1986).

While the evidence suggests that the majority of episodes of CSA are extrafamilial, when intrafamilial CSA occurs it is more likely to be characterized by recurrent or severe abuse incidents (Anderson et al., 1993; Fergusson et al., 1996). For example, Fergusson et al. (1996) examined the relationship between the severity of abuse and the perpetration of CSA. They found that while 61.3% of incidents of intrafamilial abuse involved attempted or completed intercourse, only 29.7% of incidents of extrafamilial abuse involved abuse of this severity. It seems probable that the often severe and recurrent nature of intrafamilial abuse accounts for the popular belief that the most common forms of CSA involve intrafamilial abuse because these incidents are more likely to come to attention in various ways.

STUDIES OF KNOWN CHILD MOLESTERS

In-depth information has been gathered on the characteristics of known child molesters who were attending various treatment facilities or who have come to official attention. In a review of what was known about child molesters, Araji and Finkelhor (1986) argued that research in this area suggests four broad sets of factors:

1. Emotional congruence, the most commonly cited theory about the origins of pedophilia, is that sexual abusers choose children for sexual partners because children have some especially compelling emotional meaning for them. Araji and Finkelhor (1986) suggest that such emotional congruence may arise by a variety of routes, including arrested psychosexual development and emotionally immature patterns of male socialization that may encourage dominance in sexual relationships and narcissistic tendencies in CSA perpetrators, in which they seek sexual relationships with children with whom they identify; and early exposure to sexual abuse, which may lead CSA perpetrators to resolve their reactions to abuse by becoming a CSA perpetrator.

2. Araji and Finkelhor (1986) argue that episodes of CSA arise predominantly because some individuals find children sexually arousing. It is suggested that there are a variety of routes that may lead to adults finding children sexually arousing. These include the role of masturbatory fantasies in encouraging thoughts of sex with children that may be eventually acted upon, misattribution of feelings of affection to children that may be expressed as sexual responses to children, and processes of social learning from child pornography that may encourage the view that children are suitable sexual partners.

3. It is argued in a further group of theories that individuals who engage in pedophilia do so primarily because they are unable, for various reasons, to establish normal adult sexual relationships and, as a consequence, seek sex with children as a substitute for their lack of adult sexual contact.

4. The final explanation of CSA considered by Araji and Finkelhor (1986) is that CSA occurs as a result of factors that disinhibit the individual so that he disregards or circumvents social norms and values about appropriate sexual behaviors. Factors that may encourage such disinhibition may include lack of impulse control, senility and mental retardation, or the disinhibitory effects of alcohol.

It is often believed that exposure to sexual abuse in childhood is a factor that may encourage later CSA perpetration. For example, Murphy and Smith (1996) comment,

The victim to victimizer theory of sexual abuse receives repeated attention in
the professional and popular literature. It appears that in the mind of the public
and unfortunately in the minds of some professionals, all offenders are victims
and being a victim is a direct cause of sexual abuse. (p. 181)

Despite this stereotype of the sexual abuser being a victim of sexual abuse,
the existing evidence provides only relatively weak support for this view. In
particular, estimates of the percentage of CSA perpetrators who report being
sexual abused in childhood typically range from 20% to 30% (Hanson &
Slater, 1988; Freund, Watson, & Dickey, 1990; Murphy & Smith, 1996).
There are two important implications of this finding. First, it shows that
contrary to popular belief the majority of CSA perpetrators have not been
sexually abused. Second, it nonetheless is the case that the rate of reported
CSA among CSA perpetrators is higher than in the population at large, with
CSA perpetrators reporting rates of abuse that are between two to three times
the rate reported by unselected population samples. This finding suggests that
in some individuals at least, exposure to sexual abuse in childhood may
increase the likelihood that they will later become CSA perpetrators. There
have, however, been suggestions that this relationship may reflect factors that
are correlated with CSA, including greater sexual deviancy, psychological
disturbance, and exposure to dysfunctional family circumstances (Hanson,
1990; Langevin, Wortzman, Wright, & Handy, 1989). In general, the weight
of the evidence supports the conclusion that, although most CSA perpetrators
have not been subject to sexual abuse, exposure to CSA may increase risks
of later CSA perpetration, particularly if this exposure co-occurs with other
factors that may encourage CSA perpetration.

CONCLUDING COMMENT

In this chapter, we have examined the characteristics of children who become
victims of sexual abuse and the characteristics of CSA perpetrators. What
emerges first and foremost from this literature are the limitations and uncertainties that apply to accounts of both victims and perpetrators. Studies of
CSA victims have been limited by the use of selected clinical samples of
children known to have been exposed to CSA or the use of retrospective
accounts of adults who disclose CSA. Both sources of evidence may contain
biases that make the resulting accounts unreliable or inaccurate. Similarly,
what is known about CSA perpetrators has been provided by the limited data
(age, gender, and relationship to the victim) gathered in victim report studies

or from clinical studies of known CSA perpetrators. Again, such studies may contain biases that lead to inaccurate or unreliable accounts of the characteristics of CSA perpetrators. Within the limitations that apply to research in this area, the following major conclusions emerge.

1. CSA is not confined to females, and estimates suggest that typically a quarter to a third of CSA victims are males. It is also possible that CSA in males may be underreported relative to the reporting of CSA by females.

2. Children at greatest risk of CSA appear to come from families characterized by multiple sources of difficulty and dysfunction that may span marital conflict, parental separation, stepparenthood, parental psychopathology, and impaired parent-child relationships. The ways in which these factors increase individual vulnerability to CSA are not yet entirely clear, but it may be suggested that these features increase risks of CSA by creating social environments and social ecologies in which children are not adequately protected against CSA incidents.

3. Although children at risk of CSA often come from family backgrounds marked by various difficulties and dysfunction, it is by no means the case that the presence of CSA can be inferred or predicted from knowledge of family and social circumstances. The use of family, social, or related information to identify or diagnose children as being at risk of CSA is likely to be potentially misleading.

4. Until recently, it was believed that there was a virtual male monopoly among CSA perpetrators. This view appears to have arisen because of a gender bias in the literature on CSA as a result of an emphasis on CSA in female populations. While there is clear evidence to suggest that there is a virtual male monopoly among the perpetrators of CSA involving females, recent evidence suggests that roughly one in five perpetrators of CSA incidents involving male victims are female. The estimates presented in this chapter suggest that, when all incidents of CSA are considered, 90% of perpetrators are male and 10% are female, with the great majority of female perpetrators being involved in incidents of CSA with male children.

5. Contrary to popular belief, the majority of episodes of CSA do not involve family members but, rather, are committed by other acquaintances who are known to the victim. However, there is evidence to suggest that incidents of CSA involving family members more often tend to be severe and to involve recurrent abuse and intercourse. Although abuse by parent figures

is uncommon, evidence suggests that stepparents are at far higher risk of being perpetrators than natural parents.

6. Clinical research into pedophilia has produced a somewhat confused and uneven body of evidence about the characteristics of this group. The most systematic account of this evidence is provided by Finkelhor and his associates' view that the factors contributing to CSA perpetration relate to circumstances that encourage (a) emotional congruence between the perpetrator and children, (b) the perpetrator finding children sexual arousing, (c) factors that block or prevent the CSA perpetrator from forming satisfactory relationships with adults, and (d) disinhibition that may encourage perpetrators to engage in sexual behavior with children.

7. Contrary to popular belief, the majority of CSA perpetrators have not been sexually abused as children, with estimates suggesting that between 20% and 30% of CSA perpetrators disclose exposure to sexual abuse during their own childhood. However, it is possible that for some individuals, exposure to CSA may encourage later CSA perpetration, particularly if childhood exposure co-occurs with other factors that may underlie or encourage later sexual abuse.

4

THE EFFECTS OF CHILDHOOD
SEXUAL ABUSE ON CHILDREN

A key issue in this field concerns the extent to which CSA leads to subsequent psychological damage and adjustment difficulties during childhood. There is little doubt that children exposed to CSA find this experience bewildering, upsetting, or distressing (Beitchman, Zucker, Hood, da Costa, & Akman, 1991; Kendall-Tackett, Williams, & Finkelhor, 1993). In this chapter, we review the evidence on the impact of CSA on child adjustment. Three central questions underlie this analysis. First, to what extent does exposure to CSA lead to the onset of problem behaviors and difficulties in children? Second, what factors influence the resilience of children exposed to CSA? Third, to what extent does treatment of CSA reduce the adverse effects of CSA on children?

CSA AND CHILDHOOD ADJUSTMENT

Until recently, there has been little attention given to the impact of CSA on children, with most of the research being concerned with the harmful effects of CSA that manifest in later life (Kendall-Tackett et al., 1993). There are, however, a growing number of studies that examine the extent to which children exposed to CSA are at an increased risk of a range of subsequent adjustment difficulties. The majority of studies have used research designs in which a sample of children known to have been sexually abused has been contrasted with a sample of nonabused children.

A study conducted by Mannarino, Cohen, and Gregor (1989) is typical of research in this area. Three groups of girls were selected for study: (a) those known to have been sexually abused and who had been referred to a regional rape crisis center ($n = 94$); (b) those who were attending an outpatient psychiatric clinic but who had not been sexually abused ($n = 84$); and (c) a control group selected from two schools ($n = 75$). Each group was assessed on a series of self- and parent-report measures of behavioral and emotional functioning. Contrasts between the three groups suggested that, when compared with normal controls, sexually abused girls had consistently higher mean levels of all parental reported behavior problems and also had lower mean levels of parent-reported social competence. However, with the exception that sexually abused girls had significantly higher levels of sexual problems than the clinic controls, girls who had been sexually abused showed a similar profile of behavior problems and social competence to the clinic-referred group. Mannarino et al. concluded that "this study and other recent investigations have demonstrated that sexually abused children manifest a wide variety of emotional and behavioral problems" (p. 449).

The majority of studies employing similar methodologies report higher rates of a wide range of adjustment difficulties in children exposed to CSA. Kendall-Tackett et al. (1993) reviewed a series of 26 studies that examined the linkages between CSA and a wide range of adjustment difficulties. Table 4.1 provides a summary of their findings. The table shows (a) the range of childhood outcomes studied, (b) the number of studies that examined this issue, and (c) the number of studies finding elevated rates of adjustment problems among those exposed to CSA. The results in this table make it abundantly clear that the majority of studies that have compared children known to be sexually abused with nonabused control participants have found higher rates of adjustment problems among the abused children, with these problems spanning mental health symptoms, low self-esteem, and problem behaviors including aggression, delinquency, and sexualized behavior.

In an extension of their analysis, Kendall-Tackett et al. (1993), using meta-analytic techniques, examined the associations between sexual abuse status (abused versus not abused) and a series of outcomes, including aggression, anxiety, depression, withdrawn behavior, sexualized behaviors, and internalizing and externalizing behavior problems. In their analysis, they estimated the percentage of variance in each outcome that could be explained from a knowledge of sexual abuse status. This analysis suggested the presence of moderate to strong associations between abuse status and outcomes, with variance-explained estimates ranging from 15% for anxiety to 43% for aggression and sexualized behaviors. However, percentage variance estimates are difficult to interpret in clinically meaningful ways, and it would be of interest to know how many more times likely children exposed to CSA are to develop given outcomes when compared with nonabused children. This may be achieved by computing the odds ratio between abuse status (abused

TABLE 4.1 Summary of Studies Comparing Rates of Problems Among
Children Exposed to CSA and Controls

Outcome	Number of Studies	Number (%) Reporting Significantly Higher Rates of Problems Among Children Exposed to CSA Than Among Controls
Anxiety	8	5 (62.5)
Fear	5	5 (100)
Posttraumatic stress disorder		
Nightmares	1	1 (100)
General	1	1 (100)
Depression		
Depressed	11	10 (90.9)
Withdrawn	11	11 (100)
Suicidal	1	0 (0)
Poor self-esteem	6	3 (50)
Somatic complaints	11	9 (81.8)
Mental illness		
Neurotic	2	2 (100)
Other	7	6 (85.7)
Aggression		
Aggressive antisocial	11	10 (90.9)
Cruel	2	2 (100)
Delinquent	6	6 (100)
Inappropriate sexual behavior	8	8 (100)
School/learning problems	6	5 (83.3)
Behavior problems		
Hyperactivity	7	5 (71.4)
Regression/immaturity	2	2 (100)
Running away	1	1 (100)
General	2	2 (100)
Self-injurious behavior	1	1 (100)
Composite symptoms		
Internalizing	8	8 (100)
Externalizing	7	7 (100)

SOURCE: Derived from Kendall-Tackett et al. (1993).

versus not abused) and outcome risks. Unfortunately, many studies that were reported in this literature do not present data in a way that permits an estimation of odds ratios. However, we will now review three studies that permit (from a secondary analysis of published data) an estimation of odds ratios between abuse status and outcome risks.

Einbeder and Friedrich (1989) compared a series of 46 sexually abused girls identified through agency and private therapist referrals with a group of comparison control girls who had never been known or suspected to have been sexually abused. The two groups were matched for age, ethnicity, family income, and family constellation. The two groups were then compared on a series of measures of intelligence, mental health, and social functioning. The main analyses of this data compared mean scores of the two groups and showed that sexually abused children scored significantly higher on measures of sexual preoccupation as well as cognitive, social, and emotional impairment. As part of the analysis, the authors reported rates of clinical impairment on measures of externalizing and internalizing behaviors. From this analysis, it is possible to deduce that those exposed to CSA had odds of externalizing disorders that were 7.3 times higher than those who were not exposed to CSA and odds of internalizing disorders that were 5.2 times higher than those not exposed to CSA.

Similarly, Deblinger, McLeer, Atkins, Ralphe, and Foa (1989) compared rates of sexualized behaviors in two groups of inpatients in an acute psychiatric unit: 29 children who had been sexually abused and 29 children who had not been. From the data presented in this paper, it was possible to compute the odds ratio between sexual abuse status and two measures of sexual behavior: inappropriate sexual behavior and sexually abusive behavior toward younger children. This analysis showed that in comparison with psychiatric inpatients who were not known to have been sexually abused, inpatients with a history of sexual abuse had rates of sexually abusive behavior to other children that were 12.6 times higher and rates of sexually inappropriate behaviors that were 45.8 times higher.

Finally, Gomes-Schwartz, Horowitz, Cardarelli, and Sauzier (1990) examined a range of measures of mental health and personal adjustment in a sample of 58 children, ages 7-13 years, who were referred for treatment after sexual abuse. Personal adjustment was assessed using the Louisville Behavior Checklist. Although the study design did not include the assessment of a nonabused control group, the authors were able to compare levels of adjustment in the sexually abused group with population norms for the Louisville Behavior Checklist, and it was possible from secondary analyses of the data to compute odds ratios between abuse status and risks of behavioral disturbance. These calculations produced a total of 10 odds ratios that ranged from 1.9 to 44.1, with a median value of 7.8, and clearly indicated that children who were receiving treatment for sexual abuse had elevated risks of a wide range of personal, social, and behavioral problems.

This evidence clearly suggests that children who are known to have been sexually abused are an "at risk" population for a wide range of disorders and adjustment difficulties, and at first sight the evidence suggests the presence of a causal link (Green, 1993; Kendall-Tackett et al., 1993). In the next section, we review some of the difficulties and uncertainties that arise in interpreting this evidence.

Is There a Causal Relationship Between CSA Exposure and Childhood Adjustment?

The evidence previously reviewed in this chapter provides a generally compelling case for children exposed to CSA having an increased risk of adjustment problems, which is consistent with CSA causing those adjustment problems. However, there are a number of alternative explanations of these associations. The major threats to the validity of a causal hypothesis include the following:

1. *The effects of sample selection processes.* In all studies to date, contrasts have been made between children who are known to have been sexually abused and a nonabused control group. In all cases, samples of those children who were abused have not been a random sample of all abused children but, rather, represent selected samples that have been drawn from agency records and other similar sources. The major liability of this design is that the processes by which samples of abused children are selected may produce misleading or spurious associations between CSA and risks of adjustment problems. For example, it may be argued that the heightened rates of adjustment difficulties among these selected samples arises from a bias in which those coming to agency attention are, for other reasons, more likely to have adjustment problems. This is, in fact, likely, given that the presence of behavior problems has often been the grounds for examining whether these adjustment problems were due to CSA (Corwin, 1988). The effects of this sampling bias would be to produce an inflated impression of the linkages between CSA and child adjustment.

2. *Confounding.* Even assuming that comparisons between samples of children known to be sexually abused and control series are not seriously affected by sample selection biases, there are further complications. In particular, as noted in the preceding chapter, children exposed to CSA are frequently exposed to other adverse and disadvantageous circumstances. These factors include greater exposure to family dysfunction and marital difficulties, greater exposure to

parental adjustment difficulties, and related factors. It may be argued that the elevated risks of adjustment difficulties among those exposed to CSA reflect the effects of the social and familial context within which CSA is more likely to occur rather than the traumatic effects of CSA itself. To some extent, this threat to validity can be addressed by adjusting differences between abused and nonabused children for other factors that are known to be correlated with abuse status. To date, however, attempts to control for confounding variables have been limited, with the majority of studies in this area making no attempt and others making only limited efforts.

Both sample-selection processes and failure to control for confounding factors pose major threats to the validity of inferences of causal linkages between CSA and child adjustment. Furthermore, the likely direction of study bias, to date, is to lead to an overestimation of the causal effects of CSA on childhood adjustment. It may nonetheless be argued that despite the possibility of such bias, exposure to CSA does, in fact, lead to increases in rates of a wide range of childhood adjustment difficulties. Several lines of evidence are suggestive of a causal relationship. First, there is evidence to suggest the presence of dose/response relationships in which increasing severity and/or the duration of abuse is associated with increasing risks of later symptoms (Friedrich, Urquiza, & Beilke, 1986; Sirles, Smith, & Kusama, 1989). Second, there is evidence of some degree of specificity of symptoms, to the extent that some children exposed to CSA show evidence of sexualized behaviors that appear to be a specific manifestation of their exposure to abuse (Green, 1993). Third, there is evidence that therapies designed to address CSA in children appear to lead to reductions in psychiatric symptoms and adjustment problems (Finkelhor & Berliner, 1995). In addition, both clinical experience (Briere, 1992; Trepper & Barrett, 1989) and a growing number of biographical accounts of child abuse survivors (Herman, 1981; McGregor, 1994) have highlighted the way in which CSA experiences may have profound impacts on childhood and adult adjustment.

Is There a Behavioral Syndrome That Characterizes the Sexually Abused Child?

Some of the uncertainties about the causal linkages between CSA and child adjustment noted previously would be reduced if it could be shown that exposure to sexual abuse is associated with a characteristic pattern of symptoms that is specific to exposure to CSA. Furthermore, the identification of a child sexual abuse syndrome could prove valuable in diagnosing and detecting cases of CSA. These considerations have led a number of authors to propose a specific CSA syndrome frequently linked to posttraumatic stress disorder (PTSD) (e.g., Goodwin, 1985; Kiser et al., 1988). PTSD is a condition that reflects a response to extreme and traumatic stress that is characterized by intense fear, helplessness, or horror; persistent reexperience of the traumatic event; persistent avoidance of stimuli associated with the trauma and a numbing of general responsiveness; and persistent symptoms of increased arousal (American Psychiatric Association, 1994). As may be seen from Table 4.1, what distinguishes children exposed to CSA is not the presence of a clearly defined set of symptoms but, rather, a diffuse and generalized vulnerability to be at increased risk of a wide range of symptoms. In this respect, the behavioral profiles of children exposed to CSA have considerable similarity to the behavioral profiles associated with a wide range of childhood adversities and difficulties.

The view that CSA has specific consequences that can be used to identify those children who are abused has also occurred in a forensic context, in which those giving expert testimony may argue that the presence of a specific set of symptoms is consistent with the view that the child has been sexually abused. Such expert testimony may mislead lay juries into accepting that since the child shows a particular pattern of symptoms, it is very likely that she or he was abused. This interpretation is not consistent with the available evidence for at least two reasons. First, a substantial minority of children who are sexually abused do not show behavioral symptoms. Studies have suggested that in the region of one fifth to one half of children known to be sexually abused are apparently asymptomatic. Second, with the exception of PTSD symptoms that are clearly consequent on sexual trauma or sexualized behaviors that are likely to be a reflection of adult-child sexual contacts, the pattern of symptoms typically displayed by sexually abused children differs little from the symptom patterns exhibited by children who are exposed to a wide range of social, family, and related adversities (Green, 1993). The theory that sexually abused children typically exhibit a characteristic syndrome is both empirically unfounded and has the potential to mislead and confuse in debates over the identification of CSA.

RESILIENCY TO CSA

A substantial minority of children known to have been exposed to CSA do not develop significant adjustment difficulties. Estimates of the number of asymptomatic children among those known to have been sexually abused have ranged from as low as 21% (Conte & Schuerman, 1987a; 1987b) to as high as 49% (Caffaro-Rouget, Lang, & van Santen, 1989). There are three possible reasons for the presence of these groups of apparently asymptomatic children exposed to CSA (Kendall-Tackett et al., 1993). First, it may reflect shortcomings in the assessment of adjustment because investigators may not have examined a full range of symptoms or may have failed to measure these adequately. Second, it could be suggested that the presence of asymptomatic children may reflect the presence of so-called sleeper effects, in which some children exposed to CSA will eventually develop symptoms that are not evident at the time of assessment. Third, it may be that there are a number of children who are resilient to CSA exposures and do not develop adjustment difficulties in response to these experiences.

Research into what may make children resilient to CSA is limited, but there have been a number of suggestions about such resilience factors, including the following:

1. Behavior problems are most likely to develop in those for whom the exposure to CSA was severe, of lengthy duration, or involved violence or coercive behaviors. Conversely, the development of adjustment difficulties is least likely in CSA exposures that are less severe, noncoercive, and of limited duration (Friedrich et al., 1986; Sirles et al., 1989).

2. The extent of family support, and particularly maternal support, may be influential in determining responses to CSA exposure. Those most likely to show adjustment problems in response to CSA come from families offering limited support and nurturance, whereas those least likely to exhibit these responses tend to come from supportive and nurturant family backgrounds (Everson, Hunter, Runyan, Edelsohn, & Coulter, 1989; Oates, O'Toole, Lynch, Stern, & Cooney, 1994; Waterman & Kelly, 1993).

3. The child's attitudes and coping skills may play a role in exacerbating or mitigating the effects of abuse exposure (Kendall-Tackett et al., 1993). Children with negative attitudes and limited skills are most likely to develop adjustment difficulties, whereas children with positive attitudes and good coping skills are least likely to develop problems.

From this list, it is apparent that the profile of the child most likely to exhibit adjustment difficulties in response to CSA exposure portrays a child who has been exposed to extreme and traumatic abuse, who is reared in a nonsupportive and non-nurturant family, and who has negative attitudes and limited coping skills. Conversely, the child most likely to survive CSA has been exposed to less traumatic and/or coercive abuse, has been reared in a supportive and nurturant family environment, and has positive attitudes and good coping skills.

An issue related to this is the extent to which responses to CSA are influenced by the child's gender. In particular, there have been ongoing suggestions that there are gender differences in the nature of children's responses following CSA, with males being more prone to exhibit antisocial and aggressive responses and females more likely to develop depression, anxiety, and internalizing responses (Friedrich, Bielke, & Urquiza, 1987; Friedrich et al., 1986; Rogers & Terry, 1984; Summit, 1983). These gender differences may not, however, be specific to CSA for they appear to mirror gender differences in adjustment problems among children irrespective of whether or not they have been exposed to CSA. In addition,it should be noted that Finkelhor (1990), in his review of the literature, emphasized that "perhaps the major [finding] . . . is the relative similarity of the response of boys to that of girls" (p. 325).

THE TREATMENT OF CHILDREN EXPOSED TO CSA

Increasing recognition of the prevalence of CSA and the effects of CSA on childhood adjustment has led to a rapid growth of therapies, treatments, and policies designed to meet the needs of children who have been sexually abused. For example, on the basis of U.S. data, Finkelhor and Berliner (1995) suggest that up to three quarters of children identified as being sexually abused are provided with some form of therapy. The rapid growth of therapies in this area has resulted in a situation in which strong claims are made about the need for, and benefits of, treatment for abused children, yet relatively little research has systematically evaluated the extent to which treatment is effective.

The best method of examining treatment efficacy is through the use of a clinical trial in which a number of children are assigned at random to a specified form of treatment and others are assigned at random to a control condition that does not include the treatment of interest. In the area of CSA, there are clearly ethical problems that arise in the use of randomized trials. They center around the extent to which it is ethically justifiable to expose children to what may be less-than-optimal therapy in the interests of science. For this reason, there have been relatively few attempts to assess the efficacy of CSA treatment by using randomized trials. A number of approaches have used somewhat weaker designs to examine the efficacy of CSA treatment. In an analysis of the effectiveness of treatment for children exposed to CSA, Finkelhor and Berliner (1995) identified 29 studies that used one of three research designs:

1. *The pretest/posttest design.* The majority of studies evaluating CSA treatment have employed a pretest/posttest design in which the symptom levels of children at the point of entry to treatment are compared with symptom levels following treatment. Evidence of a reduction in symptom levels is taken as indicative of possible treatment benefit. In their analysis, Finkelhor and Berliner (1995) identified a series of 17 studies that had evaluated a range of CSA therapies that included music therapy, group therapy, cognitive behavioral therapy, and other therapies. In all but one study, significant improvement in symptoms was reported for at least one outcome, assessed at follow-up periods ranging from 9 weeks to 12 months. A recent meta-analysis conducted by Reeker, Ensing, and Elliott (1997) examined the extent of pretreatment/posttreatment differences in 15 studies of treatment for CSA. These authors found that across all studies, test scores improved by an average of .78 standard deviations, suggesting clear and statistically significant improvements in symptom levels and other outcomes following therapy.

However, the pretest/posttest design provides only very weak evidence of treatment efficacy for at least two reasons. First, apparent improvements in symptoms following treatment may not reflect therapeutic benefits but rather may reflect naturally occurring remission of symptoms with the passage of time. Second, it is possible that apparent changes may reflect design artifacts that arise from retest effects. It has been well documented in many longitudinal studies that on the first administration of symptom or other inventories participants tend to report higher levels of symptoms than at subsequent administrations. The best that may be concluded from pretest/posttest studies is that most CSA therapies appear to meet the bare minimum condition for therapeutic efficacy, in that participants appear to improve following treatment; however, this does not establish that the treatment was necessarily instrumental in producing this change.

2. *Quasi-experimental designs.* These designs capitalize on the fact that not all children known to have been sexually abused receive therapy, and, therefore, it can be reasoned that those not receiving therapy may be a control group by which the benefits for those receiving therapy can be evaluated. However, the difficulty with this design is that participants may be assigned to treatment and no-treatment conditions by selective processes that may also be related to later outcomes. More generally, there is no guarantee that the treated and untreated groups are equivalent and would be expected to have similar outcomes. To some extent, these issues can be addressed by adjusting differences in group outcome for known factors that influence treatment-group membership using the so-called nonequivalent groups design. Finkelhor and Berliner (1995) identified five studies employing quasi-experimental designs, with two of these studies reporting benefits for treatment.

3. *Experimental studies.* Finally, Finkelhor and Berliner (1995) identified three experimental studies employing randomized or matched-group designs. In general, these studies found that participants exposed to treatment showed benefit. In addition, Finkelhor and Berliner (1995) reported on five studies in which alternative forms of CSA treatment were contrasted. In general, these studies found few differences in treatment outcome for different groups, although Cohen and Mannarino (1996) reported that structured, abuse-specific therapy has advantages over psychotherapy.

Since the publication of Finkelhor and Berliner's (1995) review, there have been a number of other evaluations of CSA treatment that have used pretest/ posttest designs or quasi-experimental or experimental designs (Hyde, Bentovim, & Monck, 1995; McGain & McKinzey, 1995). In general, these studies have supported the view that treatment of children exposed to CSA is beneficial. One study that is of particular interest was reported by McGain and McKinzey (1995), who compared the treatment outcomes of 15 girls receiving a program of treatment and support for CSA with a matched series of 15 girls who were on a waiting list for this treatment, with both groups being evaluated six months following trial entry. This analysis showed that, although both groups had similar behavioral profiles at the point of trial entry, those exposed to treatment showed clear reductions in the levels of adjustment problems assessed at six months. In contrast, the untreated group showed less change in behavior outcomes, and there were significant differences between the mean scores of the treated and untreated groups in nearly all comparisons made.

Although accumulating evidence now suggests that the treatment of children exposed to CSA has beneficial effects, this evidence is marked by a number of weaknesses that have included (a) the use of small and often highly selected groups of children, (b) an emphasis on the treatment of sexually abused girls, (c) a lack of studies in which individuals have been assigned randomly to treatment and control groups, and (d) limited information on the extent to which different therapeutic regimes have beneficial effects. It is clear that although the available evidence supports the conclusion that CSA therapy for sexually abused children is beneficial, the evidence for therapeutic benefit still falls far short of the standards demanded for the proof of benefit in many other areas. Many of these uncertainties could be resolved by a number of well-designed randomized trials in which relatively large numbers of children were assigned at random to different treatment options (including no treatment), with the outcomes of treatment being assessed using standardized and validated outcome measures.

Aside from the issue of treatment efficacy, there are further issues in the treatment of CSA that merit comment. It is important to note that CSA is not a disorder but a putative cause of disorder. This issue comes into clear relief when the problems of providing therapy to sexually abused children who are asymptomatic are considered. First, it is clear that with asymptomatic children it becomes difficult, if not impossible, to show therapeutic benefit since these children do not have symptoms that require resolution. Second, it may be asked whether treatment is appropriate for children who are asymptomatic. Nonetheless, Finkelhor and Berliner (1995) argue that, at present, it is prudent to include asymptomatic children in treatment and treatment studies.

CONCLUDING COMMENT

In this chapter, we have examined a series of issues relating to the impact of CSA on childhood adjustment. The following major conclusions emerge from this analysis:

1. There is little doubt that children who are known to have been sexually abused are a high-risk population who show a generalized vulnerability to a wide range of behavior problems, mental health disorders, and adjustment difficulties.

2. It is probable, but by no means certain, that the elevated risk of adjustment difficulties seen in these children can be attributed, at least in part,

to their exposure to CSA. However, it is also likely that existing research may overestimate the impact of CSA on children as a result of research artifacts arising from both sample selection and failure to control for confounding influences.

3. There is little evidence to suggest that children exposed to CSA show a core syndrome that is characteristic of CSA. For these reasons, attempts to diagnose or infer the presence of CSA on the basis of the child's symptom patterns are likely to be ineffective and potentially misleading. Children who are sexually abused typically show symptom patterns that are characteristic of children exposed to a wide range of childhood and family adversities. Possible exceptions to those conclusions exist for the small minority of CSA victims who show highly specific symptoms reflecting either clear and specific responses to sexual trauma or precocious sexual behaviors that are likely to have been learned in the context of the CSA episode.

4. A substantial minority of children appear to be resilient to the effects of CSA exposure and to be asymptomatic. Factors influencing resilience to abuse include the severity of the abuse incident, the extent of family support and nurturance, and the child's attitudes and coping skills. Those most likely to develop adjustment difficulties following CSA exposure are children exposed to severe and coercive episodes of abuse, those reared in nonsupportive or non-nurturant family environments, and those with negative attitudes and poor coping skills.

5. There has been a rapid growth in therapies for sexually abused children, but the evidence for the efficacy of these therapies is far from compelling. Although the weight of the evidence suggests that therapy for CSA may be effective, there is a need for larger and better-designed evaluations of therapy before this conclusion can be supported.

6. Sexual abuse treatment for children is complicated by the fact that what is being treated is not a disorder but, rather, a putative cause of disorder. This poses difficulties defining the objectives of the treatment, assessing treatment outcomes, and making decisions about the appropriate treatment and management of the substantial minority of children who are asymptomatic.

5

THE EFFECTS OF CHILDHOOD
SEXUAL ABUSE ON ADULTS

This chapter examines the extent to which sexual abuse in childhood influences the longer-term social and psychological functioning of those exposed to abuse. The account presents (a) a review of the evidence on the linkages between CSA and later functioning in adulthood, (b) an examination of the methodological and other difficulties in interpreting the available evidence, and (c) a theoretical overview of the ways in which CSA may influence long-term psychological adjustment. More generally, the chapter attempts to provide an overview of the evidence linking CSA exposure to long-term problems in adult life and a commentary on the uncertainties raised by this evidence.

LINKAGES BETWEEN CSA AND RISKS OF PROBLEMS IN ADULT LIFE

Over the past decade, an increasing number of studies have examined the linkages between reports of CSA and measures of psychological and social adjustment in adulthood. This evidence has consistently documented an association between the reporting of CSA and a wide range of adult problems. These problems include the following:

1. Increased rates of depressive symptoms (e.g., Bagley, Wood, & Young, 1994; Burnam et al., 1988; Bushnell et al., 1992; Fergusson et al., 1996; Mullen et al., 1993; Silverman, Reinherz, & Giaconia, 1996; Winfield, George, Swartz, & Blazer, 1990)
2. Increased rates of anxiety disorders (e.g., Briere & Runtz, 1988; Burnam et al., 1988; Fergusson et al., 1996; Mullen et al., 1993; Scott, 1992; Winfield et al., 1990)

3. Increased rates of antisocial behaviors (e.g., Fergusson et al., 1996; Scott, 1992)

4. Increased rates of substance-abuse disorders (e.g., Briere & Runtz, 1988; Fergusson et al., 1996; Mullen et al., 1993; Scott, 1992)

5. Increased rates of eating disorders (e.g., Miller & McCluskey-Fawcett, 1993; Romans, Martin, Anderson, O'Shea, & Mullen, 1995; Wonderlich, Brewerton, Jocic, Dansky, & Abbott, 1997)

6. Increased rates of suicidal and self-damaging behaviors (e.g., Bagley et al., 1994; Beautrais, Joyce, & Mulder, 1994; Briere & Runtz, 1986; Fergusson et al., 1996; Mullen et al., 1993; Peters & Range, 1995)

7. Increased rates of posttraumatic stress disorders (Rowan, Foy, Rodriguez, & Ryan, 1994; Silverman et al., 1996) or dissociative disorders, including dissociative identity disorder (Putnam et al., 1986)

8. Increased rates of problems of sexual adjustment (e.g., Fergusson, Horwood, & Lynskey, 1997; Kinzl et al., 1995; Mullen, Martin, Anderson, Romans, & Herbison, 1994)

These findings raise the hypothesis that exposure to sexual abuse during childhood may lead to psychological, interpersonal, and social difficulties in later adult life. Although it cannot be repeated too often that a statistical association does not necessarily indicate a causal relationship, nevertheless, when a wide range of studies employing disparate methodologies all point to a common relationship, a presumption, albeit a refutable presumption, of a causal influence can be said to have been established. The evidence for CSA acting as a causal factor will be critically examined in this chapter.

To set the background for this review, it is useful to present an overview of the trajectory followed by research into causal linkages between CSA and psychopathology. The first stage of this research process has, typically, involved clinical reports that patients with a particular form of psychopathology report high levels of exposure to CSA, with the implication that such exposure may have played a causal role. Initial clinical observations are then usually followed by attempts to examine the rates of CSA in individuals with, and without, the form of psychopathology under study. Such research leads to initial estimates of the extent to which particular types of psychopathology are associated with reports of CSA. The next stage of the research process involves extending the research to examine linkages between CSA and psychopathology in unselected population samples and to assess the role of potentially confounding factors that are, or may be, associated with both increased risks of CSA and with increased risks of later psychopathology.

The research history thus represents a process in which initial clinical observations of high rates of CSA among those with a given disorder are subject to increasingly refined tests that examine the linkages between CSA and outcomes in unselected populations and also examine the extent to which such linkages may arise from third, or confounding, factors that are associated with both CSA and later psychopathology.

To illustrate this research trajectory and its consequences for the views of linkages between CSA and psychopathology, we give the following brief reviews of the history of research into two disorders that have been linked to CSA. The first example concerns the linkages between CSA and alcohol abuse, whereas the second examines the linkages between CSA and eating disorders.

CSA AND ALCOHOL ABUSE

Initial studies on the possible linkage between CSA and alcohol abuse focused on ascertaining the frequency with which women in treatment for alcohol abuse gave histories of CSA. This research suggested that women under treatment often reported high rates of CSA, but there was wide variation in these estimates. A review of 12 studies conducted prior to 1995 (Fleming, 1997) indicated that the rate of CSA among those in treatment for alcohol abuse varied from as high as 74% (Covington & Kohen, 1984) to as low as 20% (Ladwig & Anderson, 1989).

The second research approach contrasted rates of CSA among those attending mental health services for alcohol abuse and those attending these services for other reasons. This methodology gave conflicting results, with some studies finding elevated rates of CSA among those in treatment for alcohol abuse (Pribor & Dinwiddie, 1992), whereas other studies found no differences (Hussey & Singer, 1993).

These studies of clinic samples were limited in a number of ways. The most important of these limitations was that clinic-based studies were unable to estimate the extent of association between CSA and risks of alcohol abuse in unselected population samples. This issue has, however, been addressed in a growing number of studies that have examined the linkages in general population samples (Bushnell et al., 1992; Fergusson et al., 1996; Mullen at al., 1993; Peters, 1988; Stein, Golding, Siegel, Burnham, & Sorenson, 1988; Winfield at al., 1990). All of these studies have reported linkages between reports of CSA and increased risks of alcohol abuse that have persisted after statistical controls for potentially confounding factors. In addition, at least three studies have reported an association between the extent of CSA and risks of alcohol abuse, with these risks being greatest among those reporting severe CSA (Fergusson et al., 1996; Mullen et al., 1993; Peters, 1988). A recent study by Fleming and colleagues (1997) suggests that these associations between CSA and alcohol abuse may arise from a complex causal process in which (a) exposure to CSA increases the risk of forming a relationship with an alcoholic partner, and (b) the formation of a relationship with an alcoholic partner increases the risk of alcohol abuse.

The available research traces a path from initial clinical observations that often suggested strong linkages between CSA and alcohol abuse to more qualified claims, derived from population-based studies, suggesting that the extent to which CSA has an influence on the individual's risk of alcohol abuse depends both on the extent of CSA and the ways in which this experience influences other aspects of the individual's life course.

CSA AND EATING DISORDERS

A broadly similar trajectory was followed by research into the relationship between eating disorders and CSA. Eating disorders, even prior to researchers' interest in the role of CSA, had been conceptualized as responses to disturbed family relationships as well as an attempt to escape the realities of sexual maturation and the adult sexual role (Crisp, 1980). When Oppenheimer, Howells, Palmer, and Chaloner (1985) first reported very high rates of CSA in eating-disordered patients, this found a ready acceptance.

Subsequent studies among eating-disordered patients initially confirmed the original observations (Hall, Tice, Beresford, Wooley, & Hall, 1989; Kearney-Cooke, 1988; Root & Fallon, 1988), but some doubt was later cast on the link to eating disorders in general by studies that found increased rates of CSA predominantly in bulimic syndromes (Vanderlinden, Vandereycken, van Dyck, & Vertommen, 1993). Rorty, Yager, and Rossotto (1994) investigated a group of 40 patients with bulimia and 40 matched controls and found higher rates of reported sexual, physical, and emotional abuse among the patient group. Contrary to expectations, sexual abuse was only predictive of bulimia when considered in combination with the other forms of abuse. Studies that compared eating-disordered patients with other mental health patients have tended to find that, although both groups reported more abuse than community controls, no significant differences existed between the rates of CSA among eating-disordered patients and other patients (Finn, Hartmann, Leon, & Lawson, 1986; Steiger & Zanko, 1990). This suggested the possibility of a nonspecific link between abuse and adult mental health problems rather than the highly specific relationship claimed by some authorities (Herman, 1992).

Studies based on random community studies have produced variable conclusions, with Bushnell et al. (1992) failing to find a significant association and Mullen et al. (1993) and Wonderlich et al. (1996) reporting a clear link. Mullen et al. (1996), in a subsequent analysis that also examined the influence of physical and emotional abuse, reported that all three forms of abuse showed the unadjusted odds ratios for the presence of an eating disorder to be greater than 2.5, but when a logistic regression was carried out, controlling for the more obvious confounding influences in the family and social backgrounds, only sexual and emotional abuse retained a significant association but at a markedly reduced level.

The initial hope of finding in histories of sexual abuse a central and specific etiologic influence on eating disorders has been, if not totally disappointed, at least downgraded. It seems, on current evidence, that CSA may well play a role in sensitizing victims to resort to disordered eating in adolescence but that the influence is neither specific nor central and often functions through interaction with other developmental difficulties.

We now turn our attention to the question of the extent to which recent research supports the view that exposure to CSA plays a causal role in the development of a wide range of psychopathological conditions in adults.

A REVIEW OF RECENT STUDIES ON THE LONG-TERM IMPACT OF CSA

The evidence on statistical linkages between CSA and the long-term deleterious effects in general population samples is reviewed in Table 5.1. This table summarizes the findings of a series of 12 studies published since 1990 that have examined linkages between CSA and psychiatric or psychological problems in adult life, using data from community samples. Studies for this review were selected using the following criteria:

1. The study was based on a community sample rather than on a clinic sample.
2. The sample consisted of at least 100 persons.
3. The definition of CSA was clear.
4. In cases in which psychiatric symptoms and diagnoses were reported, these were derived from standardized instruments and measures.
5. The data were reported in a way that made it possible to estimate the odds ratio between CSA and the outcome reported. The odds ratio gives an approximate estimate of how many times more likely a person exposed to CSA is of experiencing a given outcome when compared with a person not exposed to CSA.

TABLE 5.1 Odds Ratios (95% confidence intervals) Between Childhood Sexual Abuse and Psychiatric Outcomes From Studies Published Since 1990 and Based on Community Samples

Title/Source	Study Description	Outcome	Any CSA	Contact CSA	Intercourse
Bagley et al. (1994)[1]	Random sample of 750 young Canadian males (ages 18 to 27 years). 15.5% reported contact CSA. Outcomes assessed included depression and suicidal behavior.	Depression		2.3 (1.2 to 4.3)	
		Suicidal gesture		5.1 (2.8 to 9.4)	
		Attempted suicide		17.1 (3.4 to 85.6)	
Bifulco et al. (1991)[1]	Random community sample of 236 working-class British women (ages 18 to 50 years). 9% reported contact CSA. Depression was assessed using the Present State Examination.	Depression (PSE)		5.1 (2.2 to 12.2)	
Beautrais et al. (1994)	Case control study of 85 individuals making serious suicide attempts and 90 random controls. Contact CSA was reported by 35.3% of cases and 4.4% of controls.	Medically serious suicide attempt		11.7 (3.9 to 35.1)	
Bushnell et al. (1992)[1]	Stratified sample of 301 New Zealand women (ages 18 to 44 years). 13% reported intrafamilial CSA. Outcomes were assessed using DSM-III diagnostic criteria.	Substance use disorder	1.2 (0.6 to 2.6)		
		Depression or dysthymia	2.1 (1.1 to 3.9)		
		Disordered eating	1.5 (0.8 to 2.8)		
Fergusson et al. (1996)[1]	Birth cohort of 1,025 New Zealand 18-year-olds. 10.4% of the cohort reported exposure to any CSA; 8.0% reported exposure to contact CSA; and 3.5% reported exposure to CSA involving intercourse. Outcomes were assessed using DSM-IV criteria.	Depression	5.5 (3.6 to 8.4)	5.5 (3.5 to 8.8)	7.0 (3.5 to 14.0)
		Anxiety	4.3 (2.8 to 6.6)	4.0 (2.5 to 6.5)	4.2 (2.1 to 8.2)

Study	Outcome			
	Conduct disorder	2.3 (1.1 to 4.8)	3.2 (1.5 to 6.7)	4.4 (1.7 to 11.1)
	Alcohol abuse/dependence	2.6 (1.7 to 4.0)	2.8 (1.7 to 4.5)	3.1 (1.6 to 6.1)
	Other substance abuse/dependence	2.2 (1.3 to 3.7)	2.8 (1.6 to 4.7)	5.0 (2.5 to 10.1)
	Attempted suicide	5.0 (2.7 to 9.1)	6.4 (4.0 to 11.9)	11.2 (5.3 to 23.9)
Gould et al. (1994)[1] — 292 United States family practice attendees (ages 18 to 77 years). 25% reported exposure to contact CSA. Attempted suicide assessed using custom-written items.	Attempted suicide		6.2 (2.8 to 13.9)	
Hooper (1990)[1] — 418 female British general practice attendees (ages 20 to 60 years). 14% reported experiencing some form of CSA and 3% reported experiencing CSA involving intercourse. Psychological morbidity assessed via examination of medical records.	Psychological morbidity	3.1 (1.5 to 6.4)		7.2 (2.2 to 23.9)
Miller et al. (1995)[1] — Nationally representative sample of 441 white United States females (ages 18 to 22 years). 9.3% reported experiencing CSA involving intercourse. Treatment seeking and perceived need for psychological help were assessed using custom-written items.	Needed psychological help in last 12 months			4.2 (2.0 to 8.9)
	Received psychological help in last 6 years			2.3 (1.2 to 4.5)
Mullen et al. (1993) — Stratified sample of 497 New Zealand women (ages 18 to 65 years). 51.2% reported exposure to some form of CSA; 25.1% reported exposure to CSA involving genital contact; and 6.5% reported exposure to CSA involving intercourse. Outcomes were assessed using the General Health Questionnaire and the Present State Examination.	GHQ case	1.7 (1.1 to 2.6)	2.0 (1.2 to 2.9)	4.0 (1.9 to 8.6)
	CGHQ case	2.3 (1.5 to 3.4)	2.6 (1.6 to 4.0)	7.3 (3.3 to 16.3)
	PSE case	3.6 (1.9 to 6.9)	4.6 (2.4 to 8.9)	9.7 (3.9 to 24.0)
	Eating disorder	3.2 (1.5 to 7.0)	3.1 (1.4 to 7.0)	6.7 (2.3 to 19.4)

(continued)

TABLE 5.1 Continued

Title/Source	Study Description	Outcome	Any CSA	Contact CSA	Intercourse
		Anxiety disorder	2.4 (1.6 to 3.5)	3.0 (2.0 to 4.6)	3.0 (1.4 to 6.4)
		Depressive disorder	2.6 (1.8 to 3.7)	3.5 (2.3 to 5.4)	5.2 (2.3 to 11.9)
		Suicidal behavior	20.4 (2.7 to 152.7)	26.2 (3.5 to 197.7)	74.0 (8.9 to 617.2)
Scott (1992)	General population sample of 3,131 United States adults (aged 18 years or older). 5.3% reported exposure to any form of CSA. Outcomes were assessed using *DSM-III* diagnostic criteria.	Any disorder	3.8 (2.7 to 6.6)		
		Any affective disorder	2.4 (1.9 to 3.2)		
		Substance abuse and dependence	3.1 (2.9 to 3.4)		
		Drug abuse or dependence	5.2 (3.4 to 8.1)		
		Alcohol abuse or dependence	2.1 (1.4 to 3.2)		
		Phobia	3.4 (1.8 to 6.4)		
		Depression	3.4 (3.0 to 5.8)		

Study		Outcome	Odds ratio (95% CI)
Silverman et al. (1996)[1]	187 United States female participants in a longitudinal study (aged 21 years). 12.3% reported experiencing some form of CSA. Outcomes were assessed using *DSM-IIIR* diagnostic criteria.	Major depression	6.2 (1.8 to 21.7)
		Simple phobia	1.9 (0.6 to 6.4)
		Social phobia	1.3 (0.3 to 4.8)
		PTSD	28.6 (6.9 to 119.4)
		Alcohol abuse/dependence	8.9 (3.3 to 24.3)
		Drug abuse/dependence	3.8 (0.7 to 22.1)
		One or more disorders	6.0 (2.3 to 15.7)
		Suicidal ideation	3.5 (1.1 to 11.1)
		Attempted suicide	14.1 (3.6 to 55.0)
Wonderlich et al. (1996)[2]	Nationally representative sample of 1,099 United States women (aged 21 or older). 24% reported exposure to some form of CSA. Survey items used to assess binge eating and laxative use or vomiting.	Binge eating	2.0 (1.1 to 3.4)
		Binge + counteract (e.g., laxative use, vomiting)	2.6 (1.1 to 6.6)
Zierler et al. (1991)[1]	Community sample of 186 United States volunteers (aged 18 or older). 22% reported exposure to CSA involving intercourse. Outcomes were assessed using custom-written survey items.	IV drug use	1.0 (0.5 to 2.1)

[1]Odds ratios calculated from source data in article.
[2]Odds ratios adjusted for age, ethnicity, and parental education.

In preparing this summary, 31 studies published since 1990 were consulted and the table reports on the results of 12 of these. The principal reason for studies being excluded from the review was that insufficient data were available to enable an estimation of the odds ratios and associated confidence limits. For each study reviewed, the table gives the following:

1. An account of the study.
2. Estimates of the odds ratios between CSA and various outcomes for up to three definitions of CSA. These definitions include a broad definition of CSA including noncontact abuse, a definition based on contact CSA only, and a narrow definition based on CSA involving attempted and/or completed sexual penetration.
3. In all cases, 95% confidence intervals are given for the odds-ratio estimate. These intervals may be interpreted as giving a range of values that, 95 times out of 100, will contain the true population-odds ratio. In general, it can be shown that odds ratios will be statistically significant with $p < .05$ or better, provided that 1 is not contained within the confidence interval (Rothman, 1986).

The table shows 71 odds ratios, with 65 of these being statistically significant. A commentary on the major findings is given below:

1. *Depression and CSA:* Seven studies examined the relationships between depressive responses and reported CSA. In all cases, significant associations were found, with odds-ratio estimates ranging from 2.1 to 7.0, with a median value of 4.3. This range of estimates is consistent with the view that there are moderate to strong relationships between risks of depressive symptoms and reports of CSA.
2. *Anxiety, phobia, and CSA:* Four studies reported on associations between CSA and anxiety disorders or phobias. Odds ratios ranged from 1.3 to 4.3, with a median value of 3.0.
3. *Suicidal behavior and CSA:* Six studies reported on the relationships between CSA and suicidal behavior. The odds ratios ranged from 3.5 to 74.0, with a median value of 11.5. Although the evidence clearly suggests strong relationships between CSA and suicidal behavior, it should be noted that in all cases, the confidence intervals on the odds ratios are large (reflecting the low rate of suicidal behaviors in population samples). These results suggest that although the evidence implies strong relationships between CSA and suicidal behavior, there is considerable uncertainty about the exact size of this association.
4. *Substance abuse and CSA:* Five studies report on the associations between CSA and risk of substance abuse, including alcohol abuse. Odds ratios ranged from 1.0 to 8.9, with a median value of 2.8.

5. *Eating disorders and CSA:* Three studies report on the associations between eating disorders and CSA. Odds ratios ranged from 1.5 to 6.7, with a median value of 2.9, again suggesting the presence of moderate to strong associations between CSA and risks of eating disorders.

6. *Psychiatric disorders in general and CSA:* Finally, a number of studies report on the linkages between CSA and risks of later psychiatric disorders or in seeking help from psychiatric services. Consistent with previous findings, the odds ratio ranged from 1.7 to 9.7, with a median value of 3.8.

Aside from the specific results reviewed here, the table also suggests two more general conclusions. First, the analysis makes it abundantly clear that the associations between CSA and psychiatric disorders are pervasive rather than reflecting highly specific linkages between CSA and particular types of disorders. For most conditions that were reviewed, exposure to CSA appears to increase risks of disorders by about two to four times those of individuals not exposed to CSA. The exception to this trend is for suicidal behavior, where CSA appears to be more strongly related to risk, but, as noted previously, the estimates from studies examining CSA and suicidal behavior are subject to considerable imprecision.

The second theme to emerge from the table is that there is evidence of consistent variation in odds ratios, depending upon the stringency of the criteria used to define CSA. As a general rule, odds ratios are highest for estimates based on severe CSA involving penetration and are lower for definitions based on less stringent criteria. These trends are perhaps most evident in the studies reported by Mullen et al. (1993) and Fergusson et al. (1996), both of which show increasing strength of association with increasing stringency of the definition of CSA. These results are clearly consistent with the view that those exposed to CSA do not form a single homogeneous population but, rather, vary in the extent of their exposure to abuse, with these variations being reflected in the strength of association between the extent of CSA and risks of disorder.

The review in Table 5.1 examines studies based on community samples, excluding clinic-based studies, and has only included those studies containing data that allowed calculations of odds ratios. This approach could have introduced a bias into the conclusions. Recently, Jumper (1995) reported a meta-analysis of a series of 23 studies that examined the relationship between CSA and measures of depression and self-esteem in adult life. This analysis differed from the present analysis by including studies conducted prior to 1990, by examining clinic-based studies as well as studies employing community samples, and by using the correlation coefficient as a measure of association. Despite these differences, there are clear convergences and agreements between the two reviews, to the extent that both reviews suggest the presence of pervasive associations between CSA and later risks of psychiatric disorders.

The results in Table 5.1 show the effects of CSA on measures of mental health in adults. There have been numerous reports on the extent to which CSA influences sexual functioning and other aspects of interpersonal and social adjustment in adult life. This literature has highlighted two rather different ways in which CSA may influence sexual adjustment. First, findings suggest that those reporting CSA are at heightened risk as adolescents and adults of exposure to teenage pregnancy, sexually transmitted disease, unprotected intercourse, multiple sexual partnerships, and sexual revictimization (e.g., Boyer & Fine, 1992; Fergusson et al., 1997; Gershenson et al., 1989; Gorcey, Santiago, & McCall-Perez, 1986; Mullen et al., 1994; Nagy et al., 1995; Russell, 1986; Springs & Friedrich, 1992; Wyatt, Guthrie, & Notgrass, 1992). Second, findings have suggested that reporting CSA is associated with increased difficulties in sexual adjustment and sexual satisfaction (Kinzl et al., 1995; Mullen et al., 1994). Table 5.2 provides a review of studies published since 1990 that have examined the relationships between reporting CSA and sexual adjustment in adolescence and adulthood. The studies for these reviews were selected using the same general criteria that guided the selection of studies of CSA and measures of mental health in Table 5.1. In preparing this review, a total of 22 studies of CSA and sexual adjustment were reviewed, and the table reports on five of these. As in the review in Table 5.1, the main reason why certain studies were excluded was that their data were not presented in a form suitable for the computation of odds ratios.

There is evidence in the tabulated studies of a pervasive relationship between the reporting CSA and various aspects of sexual adjustment. The table presents a total of 42 odds ratios, with 39 of these being statistically significant at the .05 level or better. Three studies examined the association between the reporting of CSA and teenage pregnancy, showing a positive association ranging from 2.5 to 5.2, with a median value of 3.3. Two studies report on the association between CSA and various measures of sexual satisfaction in relationships, with odds ratios ranging, depending on the severity of the abuse, from 1.2 to 5.3, with a median value of 3.0. Two studies report on the relationship between the reporting of CSA and the risks of sexual assault in later life, with odds ratios that ranged from 5.8 to 9.1, with a median value of 6.9. Three studies report on the relationships between reporting CSA and multiple sexual partnerships, with odds ratios ranging

TABLE 5.2 Odds Ratios (95% confidence intervals) Between Childhood Sexual Abuse and Adult Sexual Behaviors From Studies Published Since 1990 and Based on Community Samples

Title/Source	Study Description	Outcome	Any CSA	Contact CSA	Intercourse
Fergusson et al. (1996)[1]	Birth cohort of 520 New Zealand 18-year-old women. 17.3% of the women reported exposure to any CSA; 13.1% reported exposure to contact CSA; and 5.6% reported exposure to CSA involving intercourse. Outcomes were assessed using custom-written survey items.	Pregnant (< 18 years)	2.5 (1.3 to 5.0)	3.3 (1.6 to 6.8)	4.0 (1.6 to 10.0)
		Multiple sexual partners	3.0 (1.7 to 5.0)	3.5 (2.0 to 6.2)	8.8 (4.0 to 19.3)
		Sexually transmitted disease (ever)	3.0 (1.4 to 6.6)	3.7 (1.7 to 8.3)	5.1 (1.9 to 13.6)
		First sexual intercourse before 16 years	2.5 (1.6 to 4.0)	2.8 (1.6 to 4.6)	6.2 (2.7 to 14.3)
		Rape/attempted rape (15 to 18 years)	5.8 (2.4 to 14.2)	6.9 (2.8 to 17.0)	8.3 (2.9 to 23.3)
Kinzl et al. (1995)[1]	202 Austrian university women (ages 18 to 30 years). 21.8% reported exposure to some form of CSA. Outcomes were assessed using custom-written survey items.	Sexual pain disorders	1.2 (0.5 to 3.3)		
		Sexual desire/ arousal disorder	2.2 (0.9 to 5.0)		
		Orgasm disorder	3.4 (1.6 to 7.1)		
Mullen et al. (1994)	Stratified sample of 497 New Zealand women (ages 18 to 65 years). 51.2% reported exposure to some form of CSA; 25.1% reported exposure to CSA involving genital contact; and 6.5% reported exposure to CSA involving intercourse. Outcomes were assessed using custom-written survey items.	Pregnant (< 19 years)	2.7 (1.4 to 5.0)	2.6 (1.5 to 4.6)	4.3 (1.8 to 10.7)
		Premarital pregnancy	2.7 (1.6 to 4.5)	2.8 (1.6 to 4.7)	5.4 (2.4 to 12.5)

(continued)

TABLE 5.2 Continued

Title/Source	Study Description	Outcome	Any CSA	Contact CSA	Intercourse
		Separation and divorce	3.7 (1.7 to 7.9)	4.3 (2.0 to 9.4)	3.8 (1.2 to 12.3)
		Multiple relationships	3.3 (1.4 to 7.8)	3.2 (1.6 to 6.2)	4.5 (1.2 to 16.9)
		Low satisfaction with current relationship	2.0 (1.5 to 3.9)	3.0 (1.8 to 5.0)	3.1 (1.4 to 7.3)
		Sexual problems	2.4 (1.5 to 4.0)	4.0 (2.1 to 7.5)	5.3 (2.2 to 12.4)
Wyatt et al. (1992)[1]	Community sample of 248 American women (ages 18 to 36 years). 62.1% reported exposure to some form of CSA and 45.2% reported exposure to contact CSA. Revictimization was assessed using custom-written survey items.	Sexual revictimization	6.2 (3.1 to 12.2)	9.1 (4.1 to 20.0)	
Zierler et al. (1991)[1]	Community sample of 186 United States volunteers (aged 18 years or older). 22% reported exposure to CSA involving intercourse. Outcomes were assessed using custom-written survey items.	Prostitution			5.3 (1.9 to 15.2)
		Average yearly sexual partners (> 2 vs. ≤ 2)			3.2 (1.6 to 6.7)
		Sex with strangers			2.2 (0.9 to 5.0)
		Pregnancy before 18 years of age			5.2 (1.9 to 13.7)

[1] Odds ratios calculated from source data in article.

from 3.0 to 8.8, with a median value of 3.3. In addition, the results of individual studies suggest further linkages between CSA and a range of outcomes, including sexually transmitted disease, earlier age at onset of consensual intercourse, involvement in prostitution, and other adverse sexual outcomes.

This analysis suggests that individuals reporting CSA tend to be characterized by two features. First, as a group, those reporting CSA appear to be at greater risk during adolescence and young adulthood of involvement in premature, poorly judged, or potentially damaging sexual activities, and second, those reporting CSA tend to have greater difficulties establishing satisfactory sexual relationships in later life. As was the case with research into psychiatric disorders, the extent of this risk of negative outcomes appears to increase in proportion to the extent and severity of the reported CSA. It should, however, also be noted that studies of the associations between reporting CSA and sexual adjustment have been almost exclusively confined to female samples and far less is known about the relationship between a history of CSA and later sexual adjustment in males.

DOES THE ASSOCIATION BETWEEN REPORTING CSA AND ADULT MENTAL HEALTH OR INTERPERSONAL PROBLEMS REFLECT A CAUSAL RELATIONSHIP?

The evidence we have just reviewed supports the view that those reporting CSA are an "at risk" population for a wide range of adult difficulties, including mental health problems, sexual risk taking, and poor sexual adjustment. It is, however, by no means self-evident that these associations arise because the traumatic effects of CSA cause the increased vulnerability to problems of adjustment in later life. Although this is one possible interpretation of the evidence, there are potentially confounding influences and other possible explanations that merit consideration. Factors that may influence the interpretation of the empirically established associations between reporting CSA and adult problems are examined in the next section.

The Potential Confounding Influence of Childhood Circumstances

As noted in Chapter 3, CSA is not randomly distributed within the child population and is more likely to occur to children from disturbed and disadvantaged family backgrounds that expose them to dysfunctional developmental influences. These background features include impaired parenting and poor parent–child relationships, marital dysfunction, parental separation, and poor parental adjustment and psychopathology. It may be argued plausibly that the higher rates of later adjustment difficulties among children exposed to CSA reflect the family context within which CSA often occurs rather than the traumatic effects of CSA itself on later adjustment (Green, 1993; Paradise et al., 1994; Plunkett & Oates, 1990; Stern et al., 1995).

This issue has been explored in the literature on CSA, with a growing number of studies incorporating statistical controls to take account of differences in the family and social backgrounds of those exposed to CSA (Fergusson et al., 1996; Mullen et al., 1993; Paradise et al., 1994; Stern et al., 1995). The findings of these studies have generally led to two conclusions about the effects of family context on associations between CSA and risks of adult problems. First, control for confounding factors reduces the strength of association between CSA and adult problems, suggesting that, in part, the higher rate of adult difficulties among those reporting CSA may reflect the family and social backgrounds of those exposed to CSA rather than the trauma of CSA. However, studies to date have shown that associations between the reporting of CSA and later adult difficulties persist even after the potentially confounding childhood family and social factors are controlled (Fergusson et al., 1996; Mullen et al., 1993; Paradise et al., 1994; Stern et al., 1995).

At the same time, it should be recognized that control of social and contextual factors in studies using correlational research designs is necessarily incomplete because not all relevant confounding factors may be included in the analysis. Furthermore, in many studies retrospective measures of the relevant childhood factors have been used, and these may be subject to substantial errors in reporting and related areas (Henry et al., 1994; Squire, 1989). Thus, even though the weight of the evidence suggests that the associations between reports of CSA and later adult problems are unlikely to be entirely explained by the family and social context within which CSA occurs, the possibility remains that some of these associations reflect social and contextual factors that have not been adequately controlled in statistical analyses.

In addition, those who suffer sexual abuse in childhood are more likely to have experienced physical abuse and emotional deprivation as well, with up to 40% of those exposed to more severely intrusive forms of sexual abuse also being subjected to physical and/or emotional abuse (Briere & Runtz, 1988; Chu & Dill, 1990; Moeller, Bachmann, & Moeller, 1993; Mullen et al.,

1996). The risk factors for these three forms of childhood abuse are similar, which may account, in part, for their co-occurrence. The lack of a caring and protective family of origin may also directly increase the risk of sexual abuse, as it leaves children vulnerable to approaches from sexually abusive males outside the immediate family who appear to offer some form of attention and even affection. Given the clear comorbidities that exist between CSA and other forms of child abuse, studies that do not identify the presence of other forms of abuse, and control for their effects, may inadvertently attribute to the sexual abuse the effects of the coexisting physical or emotional abuse.

Measurement Bias

In all studies to date, associations between CSA and later adjustment have been based on measures of reports of CSA made by adult respondents. As we have pointed out in Chapter 2, it is unlikely that these reports give a completely accurate account of childhood experiences. This raises the issue of the extent to which imperfections in the reporting of CSA may influence associations between CSA and measures of adult difficulties. There are two quite different ways in which measurement errors may influence these associations. First, it is possible that measurement errors may lead to artifactual associations between CSA reports and measures of adjustment as a result of recall bias. Specifically, it may be argued that adults who are subject to adjustment difficulties may be more prone to recall, report, or disclose CSA as a means of explaining their current problems (Fergusson et al., 1996). This would lead to a situation in which rates of CSA among those with adult difficulties are overreported relative to the reporting rates for those without such problems. In turn, this bias could be reflected in artifactual or inflated associations between the extent of CSA and individual adjustment. Although there have been continuing concerns about the effects of recall bias on associations between reporting CSA and current distress and disturbance (Cahill, Llewelyn, & Pearson, 1991; Fergusson et al., 1996; Plunkett & Oates, 1990), there is little evidence on the extent or nature of such bias. There is some evidence to suggest that individuals who are prone to anxiety or depression may tend to overreport minor episodes of CSA. In particular, Fergusson and colleagues (1996) found that individuals who reported episodes of noncontact abuse had higher rates of both anxiety and depression and that these associations persisted after control for family and contextual factors. They noted that the finding of elevated rates of depression and anxiety in this group was not consistent with the fact that the great majority of those exposed to noncontact abuse did not find these events distressing or abusive.

They suggest that individuals prone to depression or anxiety may be more prone to report and recall minor episodes of child abuse. This tendency, however, appeared to be confined to measures of depression and anxiety, and other measures of adjustment were unrelated to reported noncontact abuse.

Alternatively, it may be suggested that associations between CSA and adult adjustment may be underestimated, owing to the fact that a number of those subject to CSA may fail to recall, disclose, or report CSA. Under-reporting of CSA would lead to bias in the odds-ratio estimates, which would cause the strength of associations between CSA and adjustment difficulties to be underestimated (Pickles, 1995). Again, it is difficult to estimate the extent to which CSA is underreported and the likely bias in odds-ratio estimates caused by this underreporting.

Sampling Problems

Although the studies reviewed here have been based on random samples of the general population, in all cases the validity of analyses may be compromised by departures from random sampling assumptions arising from nonresponse. Studies examining linkages between reporting CSA and risks of a range of adult problems have often been subject to quite sizable sample attrition owing to nonresponse. This raises the issue of the extent to which nonrandom sample loss may influence study conclusions. In general, sample bias may act in two quite different ways. First, if those participants who were lost to follow-up had a disproportionate number of CSA experiences and adjustment difficulties, these losses could lead to the true association between CSA and adult difficulties being underestimated. On the other hand, if sample losses contain a disproportionate number of participants who had experienced neither CSA nor subsequent adult problems, the associations between CSA and adult difficulties might be overestimated. Here, it should be noted that although selective sample loss poses a threat to the validity of estimates of the linkages between CSA and adjustment difficulties, it is very unlikely that these biases by themselves are sufficient to explain away the large and consistent associations that have been found between reporting CSA and a range of problems in adult life.

This review suggests that although persons reporting exposure to CSA are at higher risk of a wide range of adult problems, issues of confounding, measurement error, and sampling bias introduce uncertainty about whether these associations reflect causal relationships. Under these conditions of uncertainty, it seems reasonable to accept the conclusion that CSA does influence risks of later adjustment problems as a working hypothesis while at the same time recognizing that this hypothesis is still subject to debate and uncertainty.

There is, however, a further line of evidence that strengthens the view that CSA may have profound effects on personal adjustment. This is provided by the growing number of biographical accounts given by sexual abuse survivors about the ways in which their experiences of sexual abuse have influenced their self-perception, self-worth, and personal adjustment (Armstrong, 1978; Butler, 1978; Herman, 1981; McGregor, 1994; Rush, 1974, 1980; Russell, 1986). Although biographical accounts have clear limitations as evidence of the causal linkages between CSA and personal adjustment, the fact that both quantitative epidemiological evidence and personal biographical evidence suggest that exposure to sexual abuse in childhood may lead to increased vulnerability to a range of problems in adult life clearly implies that the persistent associations between CSA and measures of personal adjustment are likely to reflect cause-and-effect associations rather than a statistical artifact created by methodological shortcomings.

THEORIES OF THE EFFECTS OF SEXUAL ABUSE ON ADULT PSYCHOPATHOLOGY AND INTERPERSONAL ADJUSTMENT

The evidence reviewed here provides a compelling, but by no means watertight, case for the view that childhood exposure to sexual abuse increases rates of adult psychiatric disorder and problems of personal adjustment. In turn, this conclusion invites the question: By what processes does the experience of sexual abuse lead to psychopathology or adjustment difficulties in adult life? To answer this question requires a theory of how sexual abuse affects individual adjustment. There have been a number of attempts to explain the linkages between childhood sexual abuse and later problems. The assumptions of the major theoretical accounts in this area are reviewed in the following section.

Psychodynamic Theories

In his early work, Freud (1896) developed what has come to be known as the "seduction theory," in which he attributed the development of hysteria to childhood exposure to sexual trauma. Freud, at this time, recognized possible linkages between childhood sexual abuse and later vulnerability to psychiatric disorders—in particular, hysteria. He believed that hysterical symptoms, either directly or symbolically, were related to a determining psychic trauma, the painful character of which had caused it to be excluded from conscious-ness. Freud came increasingly to believe that "forgetting" was a defense against the memory of sexual trauma in early childhood. Subsequently, he developed growing doubt over whether it was possible to distinguish, in his patients, between fantasies about childhood sexual experiences and memo-ries of such events. This led to a shift in his attention from the reconstruction of past events and traumas through the uncovering of suppressed memories to the exploration of fantasy (Ellenberger, 1970). It has been claimed that Freud's abandonment of the centrality of an actual sexual trauma and its replacement by a complex theory in which infantile sexuality, fantasy, and oedipal desires interact, was a betrayal motivated by Freud's desire to obscure the social implications of the histories of CSA (Masson, 1985). This seems overly simplistic as a judgment, particularly as Freud never denied that childhood sexual traumas could be real. In a sense, Freud faced the dilemma, which is still faced today, of trying to disentangle veridical memory from reconstruction, superimposed fantasy, and the products of suggestion. It should also be remembered that Freud was focusing on memories and fantasies that were believed to have originated in infancy and early childhood and not on events originating in later childhood (6 years and over).

Attachment Theory

There have also been attempts to explain linkages between CSA and psychological adjustment in terms of Bowlby's (1951) theory of attachment. It has been argued that there may be a reciprocal relationship between parent–child attachment and sexual abuse so that, on the one hand, poor parental attachment may increase children's risks of CSA, whereas, on the other, CSA may lead to poor parent–child attachment (Alexander, 1992). In turn, the higher rates of poor parent–child attachment among those exposed to CSA could be reflected in their heightened vulnerability to later disorder. This application of attachment theory to the explanation of linkages between CSA exposure and psychological adjustment may be criticized on two grounds. First, there is now growing evidence to suggest that parent-child attachments, though of developmental importance, do not play the central role in bringing about psychiatric disorder as claimed by Bowlby (Rutter 1981, 1995). This issue has been ably reviewed by Rutter (1981), who concluded that research evidence gives only very weak support for Bowlby's position on the role of attachment in the development of psychiatric disorder. Second, and more important, the application of attachment theory to this area is limited to the analysis of intrafamilial abuse and does not directly address the issue of the linkages between extrafamilial CSA (which is the more common form) and problems in adult life.

Posttraumatic Stress Theories

There have been attempts to link exposure to CSA with posttraumatic stress disorder (PTSD) (Lindberg & Distad, 1985). In essence, this theory asserts that exposure to traumatic stress, including CSA, results in a broadly similar pattern of responses, which is characterized by initial intense fear, helplessness, or horror, and followed by a persistent reexperience of the traumatic event, with avoidance of stimuli associated with the trauma and, psychologically, with a numbing of general responsiveness and persistent symptoms of increased arousal (American Psychiatric Association, 1994). In the long term, accommodation to the stress of CSA may lead to a range of dissociative phenomena and disorders. Dissociative disorders are held to have a posttraumatic etiology (Coons, Bowman, & Pellows, 1989; Spiegel, 1994), and in patients with PTSD there may occur radical discontinuities in conscious memories of the trauma such that the memories are split off from other memories (Spiegel & Cardèna, 1991).

This theory of the linkages between CSA and adult difficulties and disorder has been criticized on two major grounds. First and foremost, the theory is poorly supported to the extent that most individuals exposed to CSA do not show a common syndrome and, in particular, do not show predominantly dissociative symptoms but, rather, are characterized by having a heightened vulnerability to a wide range of mental health outcomes (as shown in Tables 5.1 and 5.2). Second, Finkelhor (1988) has noted that this approach does not provide an account of the intervening processes by which exposure to CSA (or other forms of trauma) is translated into specific psychiatric symptoms.

The Traumatogenic Model

A comprehensive attempt to explain linkages between CSA and later adjustment has been provided by Finkelhor (1988), who postulated that CSA is linked to later adjustment by a number of processes that he describes as traumatic sexualization, betrayal, stigmatization, and powerlessness. Finkelhor describes these processes in the following ways:

1. Traumatized sexuality involves the developmentally inappropriate and dysfunctional ways in which exposure to CSA shapes a child's sexuality. The effects of this process are to disrupt sexual development and may include inappropriate

sexual behaviors during childhood and promiscuity, sexual risk taking, and sexual dissatisfaction during adulthood.

2. Betrayal involves the realization on the part of children exposed to CSA that someone on whom they were dependent has caused them, or wishes to cause them, harm. The effects of this betrayal may include depression, over-dependency and impaired judgment in interpersonal relationships, anger, and hostility.

3. Stigmatization refers to the development of a negative self-image as a result of exposure to CSA. The effects of stigmatization may include low self-esteem, self-destructive behavior, and attempted suicide.

4. Powerlessness involves two main components. First, the child's wishes are overruled and frustrated, and second, the child experiences the threat of injury or annihilation. The effects of powerlessness may include (a) fear and anxiety, including symptoms of PTSD; (b) impairment of an individual's coping skills; and (c) a compensatory reaction that may include aggressive or delinquent behavior.

Finkelhor (1988) argues that these four processes in combination may explain the heightened vulnerability of those exposed to CSA to a wide range of adjustment problems and difficulties.

Although Finkelhor's account is superior to previous theoretical accounts, in that it attempts to develop a systematic account of the processes linking CSA to later adjustment, it nonetheless poses difficulties in developing empirical tests of its adequacy. These difficulties center on the extent to which the underlying processes of traumatized sexuality, betrayal, stigmatization, and powerlessness are amenable to observation. First, of necessity, all research into CSA is retrospective and rests on the accounts of those who are prepared to disclose CSA. It is open to debate whether those disclosing CSA are in a position to provide a veridical account of the ways in which their CSA experiences have influenced their life course independently of other factors that may co-occur with CSA. Second, even assuming that subjects' accounts of the intrapsychic consequences of CSA are reliable and valid, there are still complex problems of operationalizing and testing the theory.

CSA, RESILIENCY,
AND PROTECTIVE FACTORS

While those reporting CSA are an at-risk population for later problems in adult life, it is important to recognize that not all those individuals reporting

CSA develop mental health or personal adjustment problems. Studies have suggested that in the region of 20% to 40% of those describing CSA do not have measurable adult dysfunction that could plausibly be related to abuse (Finkelhor, 1990). There are two implications of this finding. First, it suggests that the common assumption that CSA invariably leads to psychological problems is misleading and that a substantial minority of those exposed to abuse survive this experience apparently unscathed. Second, it suggests the presence of factors that may modify or mitigate the effects of CSA and increase individual resilience to CSA and its effects.

Research into the factors that distinguish between those exposed to CSA who develop, or fail to develop, long-term difficulties is still in its infancy, but on the basis of the available evidence, several conclusions appear to be justified:

1. Individuals most likely to develop adjustment difficulties following exposure to CSA are those exposed to severe abuse involving actual or attempted penetration, a long duration of abuse, and/or physical restraint or violence. Incestuous abuse involving fathers or stepfathers seems particularly damaging. Conversely, those least likely to develop problems are those exposed to various forms of noncontact abuse (Fergusson et al., 1996; Mullen et al., 1993, 1994; Spaccarelli & Kim, 1995).

2. The nature of family relationships and support is likely to play an important role in mediating the effects of abuse, with a supportive and nurturing family environment reducing risks of harmful effects (Conte & Schuerman, 1987b; Peters, 1988; Romans et al., 1995; Spaccarelli & Kim, 1995). The influence of a positive family environment may operate at two levels. First, in producing a more stable and well-adjusted child with greater resilience to the impact of the abuse, and second, by providing an environment in which the child can recover and reestablish the security necessary for normal development subsequent to abuse. Conversely, the effects of growing up in an adverse family environment, particularly one characterized by domestic violence, is to increase the likelihood of long-term negative outcomes (Romans et al., 1995).

3. The nature of peer and partner relationships in adolescence and adulthood is likely to play a protective role in the development of psychopathology, with individuals who report affiliations with sympathetic and prosocial peers, or close interpersonal relationships, having reduced risks (Romans et al., 1995). Romans et al. (1995) also found the long-term impact of prior abuse was reduced by success at high school in either academic, social, or sporting spheres.

4. There has also been interest in the extent to which the impact of exposure to CSA may be modified or ameliorated by a number of individual personality factors. For example, Moran and Eckenrode (1992) reported that internal locus of control and high self-esteem were factors that acted to reduce the negative consequences of exposure to CSA. Similarly, Spaccarelli (1994) has reviewed evidence to suggest that an individual's coping style may be an important determinant of the longer-term outcomes of exposure to CSA.

5. The quality of adult intimate relationships and the availability of an adequate social network in adolescence and adult life may provide important protection against the long-term negative effects of CSA (Romans et al., 1995).

Much of the foregoing may be summarized by noting that these themes suggest that abuse is most likely to lead to problems of personal adjustment when the abuse is severe and the individual is exposed to a childhood environment lacking in social and emotional support. Long-term sequelae are least likely to occur when the abuse is mild and the individual is reared in an emotionally supportive and nurturant environment. Subsequent experiences of social adjustment and social acceptance at school, in adolescence, and in adult life further interact with the potentially continuing impact of the abuse. In addition to the effects of the social environment, it is also likely that personal resiliency may play an important role in the individual's adaptation to the experience of CSA.

EFFICACY OF CSA TREATMENTS

The rapid growth in CSA treatment has led to the development of a broad range of therapeutic approaches aimed at addressing the issue of CSA and its sequelae (for discussions of treatment issues, see, for example, Briere, 1992; Haugaard & Reppucci, 1988). It is beyond the scope of this book to provide an account of these therapies and their theoretical bases. Nonetheless, the evaluation of the efficacy of all treatment methods in this area has been hampered by the fact that there have been no systematic clinical trials that have assessed therapeutic effectiveness. To a large extent, claims of treatment effectiveness in the area of CSA have been based on accounts of clinical experience (Pilkonis, 1993) and the claims of clinicians, supplemented by a number of descriptive studies of the outcomes of those given CSA therapies.

In general, the evidence from the limited number of pre- and posttest studies available is consistent with the view that CSA therapy has beneficial effects for clients (Alexander & Follett, 1987; Herman & Schatzow, 1984; Smith, Pearce, Pringle, & Caplan, 1995). For example, Smith and colleagues (1995) examined the symptom profiles of 89 persons who were offered an individual-based therapy designed to provide a package of care for the CSA survivor. This package included the provision of a therapist and ancillary support services tailored to meet the needs of individuals who had experienced CSA. A comparison of participants before and after treatment revealed that following treatment, they showed marked decreases in symptom scores, with these decreases being consistent with the view that the therapy was beneficial. The findings of this before-and-after trial appear to be generally consistent with the findings of similar studies that have suggested symptomatic improvement in CSA survivors following treatment (Alexander & Follett, 1987; Herman & Schatzow, 1984). In general, the weight of evidence from these before-and-after studies suggests that CSA therapy for adults meets the minimum condition for therapeutic efficacy, in that clients showed symptomatic improvement over the course of therapy.

However, as we have noted in Chapter 4, evidence of symptomatic improvement following therapy provides only weak evidence of treatment efficacy because symptom changes may have occurred irrespective of the therapy. The lack of systematic trials evaluating CSA therapy appears, in part, to reflect a view that such trials may be unethical. For example, Smith and colleagues (1995) note, "We considered it impractical and probably unethical to randomly allocate clients receiving and not receiving treatment" (p. 117). We believe that this ethical position is oversimplified. The ethics of randomized trials in this area involve weighing two quite different ethical risks, including (a) the risk of clients in the control series being disadvantaged because they receive less than optimal therapy and (b) the risk that without such trials, therapies and techniques that may have no benefit and could, in fact, be harmful to patients are promoted as being effective. In any area in which new or innovative therapy is proposed, the counsel of perfection is that rigorous evaluation of therapists' claims should be undertaken before therapies become accepted and institutionalized. In the case of CSA therapy for adults (and children as well—see Chapter 4), strong beliefs about the need for, and effectiveness of, therapy appear to have outrun the available evidence, resulting in a situation in which these therapies may have been prematurely institutionalized before their costs and benefits have been adequately evaluated.

CONCLUDING COMMENT

In this chapter, we have examined the evidence for the view that exposure to sexual abuse in childhood has long-term consequences that impact on individual adjustment. A review of the major conclusions that may be drawn from this research is given here.

1. Adults who disclose CSA are an at-risk group for a wide range of later adjustment problems that may include mental health problems, substance abuse, suicidal behavior, and problems of sexual adjustment. The available evidence is consistent with the view that CSA may play a role in the etiology of these disorders to the extent that (a) associations between CSA and adjustment problems have been found to persist after control for confounding factors and (b) there is consistent evidence of dose/response relationships between the extent of CSA exposure and risks of adjustment problems. These statistical conclusions have also been underwritten by accounts of those with personal and clinical experience in this area. Collectively, the evidence provides a generally compelling, although by no means watertight, case for the view that exposure to sexually abusive behavior in childhood is associated with clear increases in risks of later psychopathology.

2. Although there have been attempts to link CSA exposures to specific types of dissociative disorders, in general, the evidence does not support this position. As was the case with childhood responses to CSA, adult responses to CSA reflect pervasive increases in the risk of a wide range of disorders rather than highly abuse-specific responses.

3. Although there has been a history of theorizing about CSA, there is as yet no clear account of the intervening processes that lead those exposed to CSA to exhibit increased rates of psychiatric disorder and adjustment problems.

4. In addition, whereas those exposed to CSA emerge as being at increased risk of disorder, by no means all of those exposed to CSA develop subsequent psychopathology, with estimates suggesting that up to 40% of those exposed to CSA may be symptom free. Factors that may influence resiliency to CSA are likely to include the extent and severity of abuse, the extent to which the individual is provided with social support following abuse, and, no doubt, the individual's own resiliency to traumatic events.

5. The strong advocacy that has characterized the area of CSA over the past three decades has led to a rapid growth in therapies and treatment

interventions to assist the CSA survivor. This growth of therapeutic remedies has not been paralleled by research efforts to examine the effectiveness of CSA therapies, and the evidence for the efficacy or otherwise of various therapeutic approaches remains weak.

6

CONCLUSIONS, CURRENT CONTROVERSIES, AND FUTURE DIRECTIONS

The preceding chapters have given an overview of a number of key issues in the area of CSA, including the prevalence of CSA, the social context within which CSA occurs, the characteristics of perpetrators, and the consequences of CSA for adjustment in children and adults. The major conclusions that follow from this analysis may be summarized by the following propositions:

1. *Prevalence:* Exposure to some form of unwanted sexual experience during childhood is by no means uncommon. Although there is considerable unexplained variability in prevalence estimates, the accumulated evidence suggests that in the region of 15% to 30% of females and 5% to 15% of males report some form of exposure to CSA. However, the prevalence of severe episodes of CSA involving penetration is lower, but, nonetheless, existing estimates suggest that in the region of 5% to 10% of children are exposed to episodes of CSA of this severity.

2. *Gender and CSA:* Although the early literature on CSA emphasized incidents of CSA involving female victims, there is now growing evidence to suggest that a substantial proportion of victims are male. Estimates suggest that in the region of 70% of CSA victims are female and 30% are male. Similarly, it was believed that there was a male monopoly among CSA perpetrators. This conclusion appears to apply to female victims, with over 95% of the perpetrators of CSA on females being males. The conclusion is less applicable to CSA involving males, and estimates suggest that in the region of one in five of those engaging in CSA with males are female perpetrators.

3. *Social Context Within Which CSA Occurs:* Unlike childhood physical abuse, which shows statistical linkages with measures of socioeconomic status, CSA is not generally associated with social class or other measures of social

stratification. Nonetheless, rates of CSA appear to be higher in children reared in families with dysfunctional features, including marital conflict, impaired parent-child relationships, parental separation or divorce, and parental psychopathology. The weight of the evidence suggests that these dysfunctional family features may create a social ecology that places children reared in these environments at greater risk of CSA.

4. *Characteristics of CSA Perpetrators:* The evidence on CSA perpetrators has been limited to data gathered from victim reports of the characteristics of perpetrators or studies of known CSA offenders who are in treatment. Both sources of evidence provide only limited guidance about the characteristics of CSA perpetrators in general. The weight of the evidence suggests that the great majority of perpetrators are male, that frequently they are individuals who are known to the CSA victim but are not family members, and that CSA perpetration by parents and stepparents accounts for only a small fraction of the total cases of CSA. Studies of known CSA perpetrators have suggested that these are frequently flawed and socially immature individuals who have a number of social, personal, and possibly biological features that predispose them to seek sexual gratification with children. Although 20% to 30% of known CSA perpetrators describe a childhood history of sexual abuse, it does not appear to be the case that most of those exposed to CSA go on to become CSA perpetrators. The extent to which the characteristics of known pedophiles are representative of the characteristics of all CSA perpetrators is unknown.

5. *Effects of CSA on Children:* Children known to have been exposed to CSA are at greater risk of a wide range of psychological, emotional, and adjustment difficulties. Nonetheless, not all children exposed to CSA exhibit these difficulties, and up to 50% of children show no apparent behavior disturbance as a result of this exposure. Childhood sexual abuse is not linked with a clear and recognizable child sexual abuse syndrome, but some children may show symptoms of posttraumatic stress disorder and sexualized behaviors that are direct reflections of their exposure to CSA.

6. *Effects on Adults:* Exposure to CSA is related to pervasive increases in the risks of a wide range of psychiatric disorders in adulthood; these conditions include depression, anxiety, substance-use disorders, conduct disorder, eating disorders, and suicidal behavior. However, by no means do all of those persons exposed to CSA develop these disorders, and estimates suggest that up to 40% of adults who disclose CSA show no psychiatric symptoms. Childhood exposure to CSA is also associated with problematic sexual adjustment, with those exposed to CSA being characterized by higher rates of sexual risk taking or difficulties with sexual adjustment.

7. *Treatment:* The increasing recognition of CSA as an important source of childhood trauma and adult suffering has led to the rapid development of vari-

ous therapeutic efforts to address the difficulties faced by CSA victims and survivors. The growth of therapy in this area has not been accompanied by a similar growth in studies evaluating the efficacy of CSA therapy and treatment, and the evidence for the effectiveness of CSA therapies remains weak.

This summary provides a synthesis of existing research and particularly epidemiological and evidence-based research conducted since the mid-1980s. This research has applied methods that have been derived from more general research areas, including psychiatric epidemiology, developmental psychopathology, and survey research, to provide a basis of empirical evidence on which to evaluate claims about the prevalence of CSA and its correlates, consequences, and treatment. Although this evidence is beginning to provide a relatively clear and consistent picture of CSA, there is nonetheless considerable room for uncertainty and debate about this evidence, with these uncertainties centered around issues relating to the reporting and measurement of CSA, deficiencies in sampling, and the control of sources of confounding.

Parallel to this empirical, evidence-based research is an alternative literature that derives from a somewhat different intellectual tradition. This literature, which is founded on the advocacy-based accounts developed in the 1970s, has sought to interpret and reconstruct CSA in the context of feminist and psychotherapeutic theories. In contrast to the epidemiological research tradition, which has sought to quantify the extent and consequences of CSA, this alternative literature has generally assumed, as a given and known fact, that CSA is a prevalent and damaging childhood experience that is largely, if not exclusively, confined to females and has sought to interpret CSA experiences in the context of more general themes relating to the position of women in society and/or to provide phenomenological accounts of the damaging effects of CSA on the psychological well-being of women.

The existence of these two intellectual traditions has laid the ground for a continuing series of controversies in the area of CSA, with these controversies involving debate and counterdebates about the extent to which certain, often strongly held, beliefs are well founded in evidence and theory. In the following section, we review a number of current controversies in the area of CSA that are all united by the common theme of being debates about the extent to which claims generated by advocacy-based theories can be supported by empirical evidence.

RECALL OF CHILD ABUSE:
RECOVERED MEMORY OR FALSE MEMORY?

The validity of research and theory in the area of CSA rests critically on the assumption that adults, when questioned about their childhood, are in a position to recall and recount experiences of CSA. This is a strong assumption, to the extent that recall of childhood events may be distorted and modified in a number of ways. Recall of these events may be influenced by normal processes of recall and the forgetting of personal autobiography; by the development of false memories and faulty reconstructions of childhood, perhaps colored by adult experience; and by the repression of painful childhood memories. The Achilles' heel of nearly all theory and research into CSA is that the measurement, description, and diagnosis of CSA rests upon potentially fallible memories of childhood experiences. There are two quite different ways in which errors of recall may afflict these reports. First, it is possible that through a variety of processes, including normal processes of forgetting or the repression of painful memories, individuals exposed to CSA may fail to recall and recount this. Alternatively, it is possible that some contexts may encourage the development of faulty or false memories of CSA experiences (Loftus, 1993; Ofshe & Watters, 1993; Penfold, 1996).

In recent years, issues that centered around faulty memories of CSA have come into prominence as a result of debates over what has been described as "recovered memory." This debate emerged as a result of a growing interest among CSA therapists about patients who presented with what was believed to be a "disguised presentation" of CSA, in which the client presented with many features common to CSA clientele but denied having been sexually abused. It was believed that in these patients, CSA had in fact occurred but, because of the traumatic nature of the abuse, these memories had been repressed, leading to abused patients denying CSA. To address this issue, efforts were made to develop therapeutic approaches that assisted patients with a disguised presentation of CSA to recall these experiences. This practice was justified on the grounds that it was critical to the success of therapy that patients recognize and acknowledge their childhood abuse (Bass & Davis, 1988).

The original intent of these recommendations appears to have been to facilitate the therapeutic process by providing a context within which clients could recover previously lost or repressed memories of abuse. However, the growing application of these methods had further consequences to the extent that patients were encouraged, on the basis of their memory of abuse recovered during the course of therapy, to both confront their abuser (who was often identified as a parent) and to seek personal and legal redress for the abuse (Ofshe & Watters, 1994; Prendergast, 1993; Schacter, 1996). The relatively tenuous evidence on which claims for recovered memory were based, coupled with a growing number of cases in which parents and others were accused of episodes of abuse that they claimed had no foundation in reality, led to the development of a reconsideration of the status of recovered memory as evidence of CSA (Loftus, 1993; Ofshe & Watters, 1993, 1994). This reanalysis of the validity of recovered memories led, in turn, to sharp interchanges and debates between those who believed that recovered memories were clear and unmistakable accounts of childhood sexual abuse (Harvey & Herman, 1994; Olio & Cornell, 1994) and those who believed that recovered memories were frequently false memories arising as artifacts of therapeutic processes that encouraged patients to reconstruct their childhood experiences of CSA (Loftus, 1993; Ofshe & Watters, 1993).

Central to the debate over recovered and false memories are a series of questions about the extent to which forgetting CSA occurs; the extent to which forgotten or recovered memories can be later recalled; and the extent to which it is possible to distinguish between accurate recall and false recall of CSA. These issues are considered here.

First, there is generally consistent evidence to suggest that episodes of unequivocal CSA may not be recalled in adult life. The study of Williams (1994, 1995) is of particular interest. She followed up 129 women some 15 years after they had as children received treatment for sexual abuse. She found that 38% failed to report the index episode when questioned in detail about earlier experiences of CSA. It should be added that of this 38%, some 26% did report having been exposed to CSA but did not specifically refer to the known index event. Thus, 12% of those known to have been abused would have been ascertained as nonabused. The strongest determinant of failure to recall was age at abuse, with children younger than 6 years being most likely to not recall the CSA.

Similarly, studies of individuals who report CSA, either in the clinical context or in community studies, indicate that a significant proportion report that at some periods in their adolescence and adult life they had "forgotten" the sexual abuse they experienced in childhood (Briere & Conte, 1993; Elliot & Briere, 1995; Feldman-Summers & Pope, 1994; Loftus, Polonsky, & Fullilove, 1994; Melchert & Parker, 1997; Williams, 1995). Estimates of the percentage of participants who report forgetting has varied from 16% (Williams, 1995) to 83% (Feldman-Summers & Pope, 1994), with most studies reporting rates between 20% and 40%. The exact meaning of *forgotten* in some of these studies is not entirely clear, but as a minimum it indicates extended periods when the individual did not bring to mind the abuse experience. The study of Melchert and Parker (1997) explored with the respondents why they believed they had forgotten their abuse for a period in their lives. Thirty percent could give no explanation of the amnesia, but 23% acknowledged that it was due to not wanting to think about it, with 18% reporting that remembering would have made them feel terrible. None of the respondents endorsed the period of no recall having occurred because they simply had no memories of it ever happening. This suggests an active process of avoiding recall rather than any form of involuntary amnesia.

Schacter (1996), in his eminently readable account of our current knowledge on memory, refers to "a social epidemic that has affected thousands of American families during the 1990's" (p. 249), which typically involves an adult, usually a young woman, who recalls during the course of psychotherapy long-forgotten memories of sexual abuse, usually at the hands of a close family member. These accusations are often totally denied by the designated perpetrator, which at best leads to family divisions and at worst ends in civil or criminal court action, inflicting massive and often irreversible psychological damage on the accuser, the accused, and the immediate family. Just as accusations based on such memories divided some families, they divided both the professional and research communities, who tended to regard these accounts as either recovered memories, reflecting actual early experiences, or false memories, produced by an unholy alliance between enthusiastic therapists and vulnerable clients. Prendergast (1993) wrote, "In my view the notion that human beings could be *repeatedly* abused and then completely forget about it defies common sense . . . and is contrary to whatever objective evidence we have about how human memory works" (pp. 99-100).

On the other side of the debate have been equally powerful defenses of the capacity of therapists to bring to consciousness repressed memories that on occasion, it is asserted, provide detailed and veridical narratives of actual abuse. Most notable among these spokespersons for recovered memory is Terr (1994), who in her book *Unchained Memories: True Stories of Traumatic Memories, Lost and Found,* strongly defended "clinicians' observations" and asserted "trauma sets up new rules for memory" (p. 52). However, contrary to these claims, the main problem following trauma is an inability to forget rather than a complete loss of the memory of the event (Brandon, Boakes, Glaser, & Green, 1998). Psychogenic amnesia following trauma may occur, but usually the individuals are well aware of the gap in their memory (Kopelman, 1996).

There are claims that memories of CSA are laid down in the brain through a unique process that does not apply to other forms of trauma and that can be recovered via the sensorimotor system (Herman, 1992; Terr, 1991; van der Kolk, 1994). This remains an unproven hypothesis, although these so-called body memories have acquired considerable currency in popular writings on CSA.

Current theories of memory emphasize that memories are not replicas of the events themselves but imperfect and subjectively modified records of how we have experienced those events. Though, for example, we are usually correct about the general character of our past, we are susceptible to various kinds of biases and distortions in recalling, or not recalling, specific events. Memory is a set of tools that assists us in functioning in the present. It is not a dispassionate record of our past. Recollection is open to a wide range of influences even in so-called episodic memories, which are involved in the recall of personal incidents that uniquely define our lives. A great deal of our past is lost to recall, particularly from early childhood when the language facilities necessary for autobiographical memory are poorly developed (Nelson, 1993). The longer the lapse of time between the events and the recall, the more likely it is that inaccuracies will creep in, even for events of great personal significance (Winsgrad & Reisser, 1992). When memory fails us, there is a tendency, at least in some of us, to fill in the gaps by what is known technically as confabulation.

Confabulation, which is the making up of connecting events to smooth out the gaps in a personal narrative, need be of little significance; however, when you are put under pressure to adjust your recall to fit your own or someone else's agenda, this plasticity of memory can have more sinister outcomes. That it is possible to influence the memories of others by suggestion is established (Loftus, 1993; Schacter, 1996). That individuals involved in therapy with someone in whom they place trust and whose knowledge and authority they accept are open to influence, and potentially to suggestion, is equally clear. Equally clear, as already noted, is the sudden recall of memories long out of mind in response to an appropriate cue. The problem is how to distinguish between memories that are recovered, in the sense of brought back to mind in response to appropriate cues, and thoughts that are the products of suggestion. All too often, no clear distinction is possible. Both client and therapist may believe they are overcoming the forces of repression and revealing the true narrative of the abuse, but how much the expectations, assumptions, and theoretical commitments of both participants are producing a new construction remains in question. What is not in question is that constructed pseudomemories have the same subjective force as any other recollections. And here lies the core of the problem: distinguishing the reality that lies behind two or more conflicting accounts that are believed by each teller to be the unvarnished truth.

RITUAL AND SATANIC ABUSE

Ritual abuse has been defined as abuse that occurs in a context linked to some symbols or group activity that have a religious, magical, or supernatural connotation and where the invocation of these symbols or activities are repeated over time and are used to frighten and intimidate children (Finkelhor & Williams, 1988). Claims of ritual or satanic abuse are often linked to fears of secret societies that suborn vulnerable children to involve them in gross and extraordinary sexual and sadistic practices.

The fears of satanic abuse appear to have emerged first in the early 1980s within the context of inquiries into possible sexual abuse in day care facilities in the United States. Over 100 day care centers were investigated across the United States between 1983 and 1991; de Young (1997) examined 12 such cases in detail. They involved preschool children, with a total of 650 alleged victims and over 200 individuals initially accused. The accusations of satanic abuse only emerged several weeks into the investigations, with little, if any, corroborative evidence other than the statements of the children during interviews. In practice, the trials often amounted to disputes between experts about the specificity, or even reality, of the claimed indicators of abuse and the reliability of the statements from children in the context of the interview techniques employed. Eventually, 28 of the accused were indicted and 15 convicted, though 12 were subsequently cleared on appeal.

Despite hundreds of investigations in the United States by local police departments and the Federal Bureau of Investigation, there has never been a single documented case of ritual abuse linked to satanic murder, human sacrifice, or cannibalism (La Fontaine, 1994; Lanning, 1989). Investigations in Europe have also failed to find such evidence. Putnam (1991) notes that this disturbing failure to find any credible independent verification of satanic ritual abuse indicates a need for caution in accepting uncritical claims about this issue. Paradoxically, this lack of clear evidence has been used by some commentators to support the existence of satanic abuse (Summit, 1988). For example, Jonker and Jonker (1997) postulate that the chaotic style of disclosure and lack of consistency in accounts reinforces their credibility. For these authors, it seems obvious that people who report ritual abuse, if motivated by the need for attention, recognition, power, and even revenge, would certainly try to produce more logical and believable accounts.

There is little real evidence to support claims of widespread ritual satanic abuse of children, and these claims reflect an extreme manifestation of the tendency for issues relating to CSA to lead to strong claims based on weak evidence. This is not to say that there may not be individuals or small groups engaged in ritualistic sexual activities with children or that organized rings of pedophiles do not exist (Goodman, Quinn, Bottoms, & Shaver, 1994; La Fontaine, 1994). However, there is little sound evidence to support the claim that there is a vast international conspiracy of Satanists who engage in the systematic sexual abuse of children.

THE ACCURACY OF CHILD TESTIMONY

In cases where CSA is suspected, physical signs of abuse are evident in only a minority of children (Bays & Chadwick, 1993; Everson & Boat, 1989). Thus, for the most part, evidence of CSA is based on the child's reports of exposure to abusive experiences. The reliance of many CSA cases on the testimony of children about abuse has led to continued research into the extent to which children provide reliable and accurate testimony (Benedek & Schetky, 1987a, 1987b; Bernet, 1993; Ceci & Bruck, 1993; Everson & Boat, 1989; Steward et al., 1996). The literature in this area has tended to present two rather different pictures of the accuracy of child testimony.

On the one hand, researchers using a variety of experimental paradigms have established that children's recall of past events under interview is frequently accurate (Everson & Boat, 1989; Flin, Bull, Boon, & Knox, 1992; Goodman & Clarke-Stewart, 1991; Rudy & Goodman, 1991; Steward et al., 1996). A study by Steward and colleagues (1996) illustrates the research approach used to examine the accuracy of children's reports. In this study, 130 three- to six-year-old children attending a pediatric outpatient clinic were given a routine pediatric examination supplemented by other physical examinations appropriate for their condition. Children were then randomly assigned to one of four interview regimes and interviewed about their experiences during the examination immediately following the examination and then at 1-month and 6-month intervals after it took place. The interview regimes varied systematically in terms of the method by which information about the physical examination was obtained. All interviews were video-taped, and, on the basis of the videotaped information, ratings were then made of the accuracy, completeness, and consistency of children's reports of body touching and the people involved in the examination. The principal findings of this study were that, initially, children's reports of body touching were highly accurate but that this accuracy declined with time; that the use of interviews containing enhancements (anatomical dolls, photographs, and computer-assisted methods) improved recall; and that younger children tended to report less information than older children. This study suggested that, under appropriate conditions, the reports of young children of body touching were relatively accurate. These findings are broadly consistent with a number of studies that have reported that young children are able to report potentially threatening events with an acceptable degree of accuracy (Goodman, Hirschman, Hepps, & Rudy, 1991; Saywitz, Goodman, Nicholas, & Moon, 1991).

However, there is an alternative literature that has emphasized the potential inaccuracies and biases that may afflict the child report. This literature has emphasized two points. First, that although child reports of body touching or similar experiences are relatively accurate there is, nonetheless, evidence to suggest inconsistency and forgetting in these reports (Bruck, Ceci, Francoeur, & Barr, 1995). These considerations suggest that whereas child reports are often relatively accurate, they by no means constitute an infallible source of information about the child's experiences. In addition, concerns have been raised about the ecological validity of studies in which assessments of children have been made by interviewers following an unbiased and rigorously supervised research protocol. It has been argued that the major concerns in child-abuse interviewing have arisen in the context of debates about interviewing methods that may not have been unbiased or adequately supervised (Bruck & Ceci, 1996). Under these conditions, important issues arise about the extent to which biases in the interview situation can distort the reporting of events.

The effects of interview bias have been examined in a series of studies that involved the use of interviewing methods that included features that may bias child reports (for a review, see Ceci & Bruck, 1993). In one such study, Bruck and colleagues (1995) examined the extent to which potentially biased interviewing of children could evoke false memories of a physically traumatic event—the pertussis injection—and those involved in this event. In this study, children were exposed to multiple interviews in which they were provided with misleading information and cues about their responses to the injection and people present. The purpose of this study was to mimic a biased CSA interviewing process in which children were exposed to multiple interviews that provided repeated cues about the response being sought. The results of this study indicated that children provided with misleading information differed in their accounts of the pertussis injection from those of a control series who were not given misleading information. They were also more prone to make their reports of those individuals who were present at the time of the injection consistent with misleading information provided during intervening interviews. The authors of this experiment concluded that "the results of this experiment show that six year old children can be misled about salient events involving their own bodies when repeatedly provided with misinformation about the event after a lengthy delay" (p. 207).

In many respects, the studies by Steward et al. (1996) and Bruck et al. (1995) illustrate two alternative perspectives on the issue of the credibility of child testimony. On the one hand, the research by Steward et al. (1996) provides the positive message that, provided interviewing is conducted by impartial interviewers who carefully follow protocols designed to assist the child in the recall of past events, child reports offer relatively accurate, but by no means infallible, accounts of these events. On the other hand, the research conducted by Bruck et al. (1995) posts a clear warning that biased and repeated interviewing can lead children to make false reports of events that did not occur. Taken together, these studies clearly illustrate that the credibility of child testimony depends critically on the impartiality and integrity of the interviewing processes: Careful and supportive interviewing may encourage accurate disclosure; biased and opinionated interviewing may encourage false allegations (Benedek & Schetky, 1987a; Ceci & Bruck, 1993; Goodman & Clarke-Stewart, 1991).

CHILD SEXUAL ABUSE AND
MULTIPLE PERSONALITY DISORDER

Persons diagnosed with multiple personality disorder (MPD) are reported to have extremely high rates of CSA (Bucky & Dallenberg, 1992; Putnam, Guroff, Silberman, Barvan, & Post, 1986). The strong association between MPD and CSA is of recent origin and was not reported in the detailed accounts of MPD in the 19th and early 20th centuries (Bowman, 1990). The origins of MPD have been hypothesized to lie in repeated dissociations. These patients are peculiarly prone to dissociative states in response to stress. They defend against fear, anxiety, and depression by denying that the stressful events are happening to them (Ludwig, Brandsma, Wilbur, Benfeldt, & Jameson, 1972; Spiegel, 1994). The most common stress to begin this method of coping is now said to be CSA, usually of a severe and persistent type. These repeated dissociations are said to produce a separate store of memories that ultimately lead to different chains of integrated memories with groups of specific behaviors that can be separated by impermeable barriers—in short, the development of separate personalities (Braun, 1990).

Multiple personality disorder was first clearly linked to CSA in the celebrated case of Sybil, which was popularized first in book form (Schreiber, 1973) and then as a movie. Gross sexual abuse during childhood was the postulated origin of Sybil's MPD. Interestingly, considerable doubt has recently been cast on the authenticity of the stories about Sybil (Borch-Jacobsen, 1997). MPD, or, as it is now known, dissociative identity disorder, has, notwithstanding occasional skepticism, particularly among British and European psychiatrists, gone from strength to strength, spawning a plethora of therapists and support groups and continuing to be closely linked to CSA. There are a number of curiosities about the CSA reported by persons diagnosed with MPD: Female perpetrators (mothers, in particular) are said to constitute up to one quarter of abusers; the abuse is often claimed to have occurred before the age of 3 years; and the reporting of satanic and ritual abuse is far from a rarity (Ross, Anderson, Fleisher, & Norton, 1991; Spanos, 1996; Wakefield & Underwager, 1992). Spanos (1996) suggested there was no substantial evidence for a causal relationship between CSA and MPD and argued that "patients shape their experiences (including their memories) to correspond with understandings and expectations derived largely from their therapists but also from popular biographies, movies, television shows and other cultural sources" (p. 285). In short, MPD may be, in part, an iatrogenic disorder telling us as much, if not more, about the current belief systems of therapists than about the mental disorders of their patients.

FUTURE RESEARCH DIRECTIONS

It is clear from the foregoing discussion that over the past two to three decades there has been a steady accumulation of knowledge about CSA, which has done much to clarify issues relating to the prevalence of CSA and the understanding of the consequences of CSA for both children and adults. However, it is equally clear that despite this large research investment and the air of certainty that pervades many public presentations of CSA, there is still considerable room for doubt and uncertainty in this area. Areas that may be identified as priorities for future research include the following:

- *The need to clarify the definition and meaning of CSA.* The politicized context within which CSA was rediscovered has led to a broad and somewhat indiscriminate use of the term *childhood sexual abuse,* with this term being used to cover a wide range of unwanted childhood sexual experiences spanning single incidents of noncontact abuse to multiple and repeated acts of gross sexual violation. Although, for the purposes of publicizing the issue of CSA, it was convenient to include a wide range of quite different childhood sexual experiences within the general definition, this broad classification has proved to be a continued source of difficulty in research in this area. An important step in research into CSA is the development of a more refined and exact vocabulary to describe different types of unwanted childhood sexual experience. There are several ways in which this conceptual clarification could be achieved.

First, there is a need for a broad consensus about the domain of unwanted childhood sexual experiences that should be included in this area of study. Second, there is a need to develop typologies that distinguish between different kinds of childhood sexual abuse. Third, there is a need to develop measurement methods and techniques to describe, for each type of CSA, the extent and severity of the abuse incident. One approach that may be useful in clarifying the definition of abuse severity and extent is to adapt methods that have been applied in the more general area of life-events research to judge the stress caused by exposure to a specific life event in the context of a particular set of circumstances. In these methods, vignettes of the adverse life event are constructed on the basis of report data and, using these vignettes, expert panels rate the extent to which the life event had stressful, threatening, or distressing features (Brown & Harris, 1978). This technology could be readily adapted to the assessment of the severity and intrusiveness of CSA incidents and may provide the basis for describing the extent or severity of abuse on a systematic and reliable basis.

Irrespective of the processes by which the clarification of CSA is to be achieved, the evidence reviewed in this book clearly suggests a need for future research into CSA to move away from global definitions that classify children as abused or not abused and toward approaches that deconstruct CSA into its components of unwanted child sexual experience and also arrive at some method for assessing the extent and severity of abuse.

- *The need for a clearer understanding of the meaning and validity of recalled childhood experience.* Of necessity, research into the prevalence and consequences of CSA within general population samples will continue to rely on the reports of adults about their childhood experiences. Given the central role of recalled experience in measuring and defining CSA, it is clearly important that we reach an improved understanding of both the limitations and the uses of recalled experiences. As noted in the discussions of the debates surrounding recovered memory, false memory syndrome, and child testimony, issues relating to the accuracy and meaning of recalled experience are likely to continue to plague both research into CSA and clinical practice in this area because there is no gold standard against which recalled experience may be validated. Despite this limitation, a number of approaches may serve to clarify some aspects of report data based on recalled experience, such as the following:

1. Further randomized field trials to examine the extent to which the reporting of CSA is influenced by the methods by which data are gathered, the types of question asked, the context within which questioning occurs, and related features of data collection

2. The use of longitudinal or panel designs, in which persons are questioned about their CSA experiences on multiple occasions to examine the stability of their reporting of CSA over time and the factors associated with changes in their CSA reports

3. Long-term studies of children known to be sexually abused to determine the accuracy of later recall of childhood experiences among those exposed to CSA

4. Further experimental and developmental research into the accuracy of child testimony and the interviewing methods likely to lead to both valid and false accounts

Although none of these approaches provide a final resolution of the accuracy of CSA reports, it may be possible to reach a clearer account of both the likely accuracy of CSA reports and the potential limitations of these reports as accounts of childhood experience.

- *The need for further semiprospective studies of the childhood context within which CSA occurs.* Many of the issues raised in the study of CSA could be clarified by fully prospective studies in which the extent of CSA exposure during childhood was assessed at regular periods, together with data on family social circumstances, family economic circumstances, and child adjustment prior to and following CSA exposures. As we pointed out previously, there are nearly insuperable practical and ethical problems in mounting this type of prospective study. However, an alternative is provided by semiprospective designs in which a cohort of children is studied throughout childhood to obtain details on family social circumstances, family economic circumstances, family functioning, and child adjustment. When the cohort members reach adulthood, it would be possible to question them about childhood exposures to CSA in a way that overcomes many of the practical and ethical problems that arise in the implementation of the fully prospective design. Furthermore, this approach has two advantages over retrospective designs in which accounts of CSA and childhood circumstances are provided on the basis of adult recall. First, the semiprospective design makes it possible to use prospectively collected data to identify the characteristics of those who later disclose CSA and those who do not. Second, by using prospectively measured childhood factors in the semi-prospective design, it is possible to control associations between CSA and measures of adjustment for childhood, family, and social experiences that were present prior to the reported CSA exposure, thus providing more exact control of the extent to which associations between CSA and measures of personal adjustment are influenced by confounding social, family, and individual factors.

- *Research into ethical issues relating to collection of CSA data.* In our experience, much research into CSA is conducted against a background of concern that questioning people about CSA may have harmful or distressing effects on those who are questioned. These concerns often lead to lengthy debates about the ethics of CSA interviewing (Fergusson et al., 1996; Martin, Perrott, Morris, & Romans, in press; Merry & Andrews, 1989; Von Dadelszen, 1987). There is very little evidence to support this view, and, in general, a growing number of studies have reported that those questioned about CSA do not appear to experience harm or major distress as a consequence of this questioning (Fergusson et al., 1996; Merry & Andrews, 1989; Von Dadelszen, 1987). Nonetheless, to the extent that concerns about the potentially harmful effects of CSA interviewing form an important component of the ethical assessment of CSA research, it is vital that further research be undertaken to determine the extent to which CSA interviewing has harmful or distressing long- and short-term effects on those participating in this research. The most powerful way of conducting such research would be to set up a randomized field experiment involving a large community sample, with one half of this sample being assigned at random to questioning about CSA and the other half not being questioned about CSA. This sample could then be studied longitudinally to examine the extent to which those exposed to CSA questioning showed different patterns of adjustment and responses from those not exposed to CSA questioning. Although, on the basis of the existing evidence, it is highly likely that such a trial would show that CSA questioning does not lead to marked personal distress or adverse reactions among those exposed to CSA, the demonstration of this fact using a randomized field trial would provide strong evidence to address the concerns that appear to arise frequently when research into CSA is proposed.

- *Randomized trials of treatment efficacy.* There is little doubt that the major research priority in the area of CSA involves the systematic evaluation of CSA therapy. Over the past decade, there has been a rapid growth in the number of CSA therapies and therapists. This growth has been underwritten by the assumptions that (a) CSA has harmful effects on the individual's short-term and long-term adjustment and (b) these effects can be ameliorated by the provision of appropriate therapy to address the issue of CSA. As we noted previously (see Chapters 4 and 5), there is very little research that has evaluated the extent to which CSA therapies have beneficial or harmful effects. Given the large social and financial investments being made into these therapies, it is clearly vital that large scale and systematic trials be undertaken to examine (a) the extent to which CSA therapy has beneficial effects when compared with no therapy and (b) the extent to which different types of CSA therapy have beneficial or detrimental consequences when these therapies are compared. The best route to conducting this assessment is clearly through the use of randomized field trials, in which individuals are assigned at random to various therapeutic options (including no therapy) to determine the extent to which different therapeutic regimes have beneficial or detrimental effects.

Not only would such trials answer issues about the efficacy of CSA therapies, but they may also provide further indirect evidence on the causal role of CSA in the development of adjustment problems. In particular, if it could be shown that therapies that address CSA are superior to therapies that do not address CSA, this evidence would clearly suggest that the specific treatment of CSA reduces adjustment problems. This, in turn, would provide support for the view that exposure to CSA, in the absence of other factors, increases individual vulnerability to adjustment problems.

CONCLUDING COMMENT

There is little doubt that research into CSA is demanding and that even well-designed studies are likely to face considerable doubt and uncertainty arising from problems of defining CSA and measuring CSA experiences accurately. In general, the prospects for obtaining clear and unambiguous answers to many of the key questions in this area are not good, and for this reason the area is likely to be avoided by those research purists who focus on the quality of research design rather than on the importance of the research question. Nonetheless, given the contemporary context in which CSA has been rediscovered and the history of claims and counterclaims that have been made about the prevalence and consequences of CSA, the only route to resolving these issues is through further well-designed research to address key issues in this area. It is unlikely that any specific research study, by itself, will resolve the ambiguities, doubts, and uncertainties that will continue to beset this area; however, it *is* likely that a steady accumulation of research knowledge may aid considerably in refining the conceptualization of CSA, identifying the strengths and limitations of measures based on recalled experience, identifying the social and family contexts within which CSA is more likely to occur, clarifying the effects of CSA on those susceptible to psychiatric disorder, and, perhaps most important, examining the extent to which treatment for CSA has beneficial or detrimental consequences for those receiving treatment.

REFERENCES

Alexander, P. C. (1992). Application of attachment theory to the study of sexual abuse. *Journal of Consulting and Clinical Psychology, 60,* 185–195.

Alexander, P. C., & Follet, V. M. (1987). Personal constructs in the group treatment of incest. In R. A. Neimeyer & G. J. Neimeyer (Eds.), *Personal construct therapy casebook.* New York: Springer.

American Psychiatric Association. (1980). *Diagnostic and statistical manual of mental disorders, 3rd ed. (DSM-III).* Washington, DC: Author.

American Psychiatric Association. (1987). *Diagnostic and statistical manual of mental disorders, 3rd ed. revised. (DSM-IIIR).* Washington, DC: Author.

American Psychiatric Association. (1994). *Diagnostic and statistical manual of mental disorders, 4th ed. (DSM-IV).* Washington, DC: Author.

Anderson, J. C., Martin, J. L., Mullen, P. E., Romans, S. E., & Herbison, P. (1993). The prevalence of childhood sexual abuse experiences in a community sample of women. *Journal of the American Academy of Child and Adolescent Psychiatry, 32,* 911–919.

Araji, S., & Finkelhor, D. (1986). Abusers: A review of the research. In D. Finkelhor (Ed.), *A sourcebook on child sexual abuse* (pp. 89–118). Beverly Hills, CA: Sage.

Armstrong, L. (1978). *Kiss Daddy goodnight: A speak-out on incest.* New York: Pocket Books.

Bagley, C. (1990). Is the prevalence of child sexual abuse decreasing? Evidence from a random sample of 750 young adult women. *Psychological Reports, 66,* 1037–1038.

Bagley, C. (1995). *Child sexual abuse and mental health in adolescents and adults.* Aldershot, England: Avebury.

Bagley, C., Wood, M., & Young, L. (1994). Victim to abuser: Mental health and behavioral sequels of child sexual abuse in a community survey of young adult males. *Child Abuse & Neglect, 18,* 683–697.

Baker, A. W., & Duncan, S. P. (1985). Child sexual abuse: A study of prevalence in Great Britain. *Child Abuse & Neglect, 9,* 457–467.

Bass, E., & Davis, L. (1988). *The courage to heal: A guide for women survivors of child sexual abuse.* New York: Harper & Row.

Bays, J., & Chadwick, D. (1993). Medical diagnosis of the sexually abused child. *Child Abuse & Neglect, 17,* 91–110.

Beautrais, A., Joyce, P. R., & Mulder, R. T. (1994). Child sexual abuse and risks of suicidal behaviour. In P. R. Joyce, R. T. Mulder, M. A. Oakley-Browne, J. D. Sellman, &

W. G. A. Watkins (Eds.), *Development, personality and psychopathology* (pp. 141–148). Christchurch, NZ: Christchurch School of Medicine.

Beitchman, J. H., Zucker, K. J., Hood, J. E., da Costa, G. A., & Akman, D. (1991). A review of the short-term effects of child sexual abuse. *Child Abuse & Neglect, 15,* 537–556.

Bendixen, M., Muus, K. M., & Schei, B. (1994). The impact of child sexual abuse—A study of a random sample of Norwegian students. *Child Abuse & Neglect, 18,* 837–847.

Benedek, E. P., & Schetky, D. H. (1987a). Problems in validating allegations of sexual abuse. Part 1: Factors affecting perception and recall of events. *Journal of the American Academy of Child and Adolescent Psychiatry, 26,* 912–915.

Benedek, E. P., & Schetky, D. H. (1987b). Problems in validating allegations of sexual abuse. Part 2: Clinical evaluation. *Journal of the American Academy of Child and Adolescent Psychiatry, 26,* 916–921.

Bergner, R. M., Delgado, L. K., & Graybill, G. (1994). Finkelhor's risk factor checklist: A cross-validation study. *Child Abuse & Neglect, 18,* 331–340.

Bernet, W. (1993). False statements and the differential diagnosis of abuse allegations. *Journal of the American Academy of Child and Adolescent Psychiatry, 32,* 903–910.

Bertolli, J., Morgenstern, H., & Sorenson, S. B. (1995). Estimating the occurrence of child maltreatment and risk-factor effects: Benefit of a mixed-design strategy in epidemiologic research. *Child Abuse & Neglect, 19,* 1007–1016.

Bifulco, A., Brown, G. W., & Adler, Z. (1991). Early sexual abuse and clinical depression in adult life. *British Journal of Psychiatry, 159,* 115–122.

Borch-Jacobsen, M. (1997). Sybil—The making of a disease: An interview with Herbert Spiegel. *The New York Review.*

Bowlby, J. (1951). *Maternal care and mental health.* WHO Monograph Series, No. 2. Geneva: World Health Organization.

Bowman, E. S. (1990). Adolescent multiple personality disorder in the nineteenth and early twentieth centuries. *Dissociation, 3,* 179–187.

Boyer, D., & Fine, D. (1992). Sexual abuse as a factor in adolescent pregnancy and child maltreatment. *Family Planning Perspectives, 24,* 4–11.

Brandon, S., Boakes, J. P., Glaser, D., & Green, R. (1998). Recovered memories of childhood sexual abuse: Implications for clinical practice. *British Journal of Psychiatry, 172,* 296-307.

Braun, B. G. (1990). Multiple personality disorder: An overview. *American Journal of Occupational Therapy, 44,* 971–976.

Briere, J., & Conte, J. (1993). Self-reported amnesia for abuse in adults molested as children. *Journal of Traumatic Stress, 6,* 21–31.

Briere, J., & Runtz, M. (1986). Suicidal thoughts and behaviours in former sexual abuse victims. *Canadian Journal of Behavioral Science, 18,* 413–423.

Briere, J., & Runtz, M. (1988). Symptomatology associated with child sexual victimization in a nonclinical adult sample. *Child Abuse & Neglect, 12,* 51–59.

Briere, J., Smiljanich, K., & Henschel, D. (1994). Sexual fantasies, gender, and molestation history. *Child Abuse & Neglect, 18,* 131–137.

Briere, J. N. (1992). *Child abuse trauma: Theory and treatment of the lasting effects.* Newbury Park, CA: Sage.

114   CHILDHOOD SEXUAL ABUSE

Brown, G. R., & Anderson, B. (1991). Psychiatric morbidity in adult inpatients with childhood histories of sexual and physical abuse. *American Journal of Psychiatry, 148,* 55–61.

Brown, G. W., & Harris, T. (1978). *Social origins of depression.* New York: Free Press.

Bruck, M., & Ceci, S. J. (1996). Commentary: Issues in the scientific validation of interviews with young children. In M. S. Steward, D. Steward, L. Farquhar, J. E. B. Myers, M. Reinhart, J. Welker, N. Joyle, J. Driskill, & J. Morgan, Interviewing young children about body touch and handling. *Monographs of the Society for Research in Child Development, 61,* 204–214.

Bruck, M., Ceci, S. J., Francoeur, E., & Barr, R. (1995). "I hardly cried when I got my shot!": Influencing children's reports about a visit to their paediatrician. *Child Development, 66,* 193–208.

Bucky, S. J., & Dallenberg, C. (1992). The relationship between training of mental health professionals and the reporting of ritual abuse and multiple personality disorder symptomatology. *Journal of Psychology and Theology, 20,* 233–238.

Burnam, M. A., Stein, J. A., Golding, J. M., Siegel, J. M., Sorenson, S. B., Forsythe, A. B., & Felles, C. A. (1988). Sexual assault and mental disorders in a community population. *Journal of Consulting and Clinical Psychology, 56,* 843–850.

Bushnell, J. A., Wells, J. E., & Oakley-Browne, M. (1992). Long-term effects of intrafamilial sexual abuse in childhood. *Acta Psychiatrica Scandinavica, 85,* 136–142.

Butler, S. (1978). *Conspiracy of silence: The trauma of incest.* San Francisco: Volcano.

Butler-Sloss, E. (1988). *Report of the inquiry into child abuse in Cleveland in 1987.* London: Her Majesty's Stationery Office.

Caffaro-Rouget, A., Lang, R. A., & van Santen, V. (1989). The impact of child sexual abuse. *Annals of Sex Research, 2,* 29–47.

Cahill, C., Llewelyn, S. P., & Pearson, C. (1991). Long-term effects of sexual abuse which occurred in childhood: A review. *British Journal of Clinical Psychology, 30,* 117–130.

Carlin, A. S., Kemper, K., Ward, N. G., Sowell, H., Gustafson, B., & Stevens, N. (1994). The effects of differences in objective and subjective definitions of childhood physical abuse on estimates of its incidence and relationship to psychopathology. *Child Abuse & Neglect, 18,* 393–399.

Ceci, S. J., & Bruck, M. (1993). The suggestibility of the child witness: A historical review and synthesis. *Psychological Bulletin, 113,* 403–440.

Ceci, S. J., & Bruck, M. (1995). *Jeopardy in the courtroom.* Washington, DC: American Psychological Association.

Chu, J. A., & Dill, D. L. (1990). Dissociative symptoms in relation to childhood physical and sexual abuse. *American Journal of Psychiatry, 147,* 887–892.

Cohen, J. A., & Mannarino, A. P. (1996). A treatment outcome study for sexually abused preschool children: Initial findings. *Journal of the American Academy of Child and Adolescent Psychiatry, 35,* 42–50.

Collings, S. J. (1995). The long-term effects of contact and noncontact forms of child sexual abuse in a sample of university men. *Child Abuse & Neglect, 19,* 1–6.

Connelly, C., & Straus, M. (1992). Mother's age and risk for physical abuse. *Child Abuse & Neglect, 16,* 709–718.

Conte, J. R., & Schuerman, J. R. (1987a). Factors associated with an increased impact of child sexual abuse. *Child Abuse & Neglect, 11,* 201–211.

Conte, J. R., & Schuerman, J. R. (1987b). The effects of sexual abuse on children: A multidimensional view. *Journal of Interpersonal Violence, 2,* 380–390.

Coons, P., Bowman, E., & Pellows, T. A. (1989). Post-traumatic aspects of the treatment of victims of sexual abuse and incest. *Psychiatric Clinics of North America, 12,* 325–337.

Corwin, D. L. (1988). Early diagnosis of child sexual abuse: Diminishing the lasting effects. In G. E. Wyatt & G. J. Powell (Eds.), *Lasting effects of child sexual abuse* (pp. 251–270). Newbury Park, CA: Sage.

Covington, S. S., & Kohen, J. (1984). Women, alcohol and sexuality. *Advances in Substance Abuse, 4,* 41–56.

Crisp, A. N. (1980). *Anorexia nervosa.* London: Academic Press.

de Young, M. (1997). Satanic abuse in day care. *Child Abuse Review, 6,* 84–93.

Deblinger, E., McLeer, S. V., Atkins, M. S., Ralphe, D., & Foa, E. (1989). Post-traumatic stress in sexually abused, physically abused, and nonabused children. *Child Abuse & Neglect, 13,* 403–408.

Dell, P. F., & Eisenhower, J. W. (1990). Adolescent multiple personality disorder: A preliminary study of 11 cases. *Journal of the American Academy of Child and Adolescent Psychiatry, 29,* 359–366.

Dembo, R., Williams, L., Schmeidler, J., & Christensen, C. (1993). Juvenile detainees: A 3-year follow-up. *International Journal of the Addictions, 28,* 631–658.

Dhaliwal, G. K., Gauzas, L., Antonowicz, D. H., & Ross, R. R. (1996). Adult male survivors of childhood sexual abuse: Prevalence, sexual abuse characteristics, and long-term effects. *Clinical Psychology Review, 16,* 619–639.

Dill, D. L., Chu, J. A., Grob, M. C., & Eisen, S. (1991). The reliability of abuse history reports: A comparison of two inquiry formats. *Comprehensive Psychiatry, 32,* 166–169.

Dubowitz, H., Hampton, R. L., Bithoney, W. G., & Newberger, E. H. (1987). Inflicted and noninflicted injuries: Differences in child and familial characteristics. *American Journal of Orthopsychiatry, 57,* 525–535.

Einbeder, A. J., & Friedrich, W. N. (1989). Psychological functioning and behavior of sexually abused girls. *Journal of Consulting and Clinical Psychology, 57,* 155–157.

Ellenberger, H. F. (1970). *The discovery of the unconscious.* New York: Basic Books.

Elliot, D. M., & Briere, J. (1995). Post-traumatic stress associated with delayed recall of sexual abuse: A general population study. *Journal of Traumatic Stress, 8,* 629–647.

Elliot, D. M., & Briere, J. (1992). Sexual abuse trauma among professional women: Validating the Trauma Symptom Checklist–40 (TSC-40). *Child Abuse & Neglect, 16,* 391–398.

Elliott, M., Browne, K., & Kilcoyne, J. (1995). Child sexual abuse prevention: What offenders tell us. *Child Abuse & Neglect, 19,* 579–594.

Everson, M. D., & Boat, B. W. (1989). False allegations of sexual abuse by children and adolescents. *Journal of the American Academy of Child and Adolescent Psychiatry, 28*(2), 230–235.

Everson, M. D., Hunter, W. M., Runyan, D. K., Edelsohn, C. A., & Coulter, M. L. (1989). Maternal support following disclosure of incest. *American Journal of Orthopsychiatry, 59,* 197–207.

Feldman, W., Feldman, E., Goodman, J. T., McGrath, P. J., Pless, R. P., Corsini, L., & Bennett, S. (1991). Is childhood sexual abuse really increasing in prevalence? An analysis of the evidence. *Pediatrics, 88,* 29–33.

116   CHILDHOOD SEXUAL ABUSE

Feldman-Summers, S., & Pope, K. S. (1994). The experience of "forgetting" childhood abuse: A national survey of psychologists. *Journal of Consulting and Clinical Psychology, 62,* 636–639.

Fergusson, D. M., Horwood, L. J., & Lynskey, M. T. (1996). Childhood sexual abuse and psychiatric disorders in young adulthood. Part II. Psychiatric outcomes of sexual abuse. *Journal of the American Academy of Child and Adolescent Psychiatry, 35,* 1365–1374.

Fergusson, D. M., Horwood, L. J., & Lynskey, M. T. (1997). Childhood sexual abuse, adolescent sexual behaviors and sexual revictimization. *Child Abuse & Neglect, 21,* 789–803.

Fergusson, D. M., & Lynskey, M. T. (1997). Physical punishment/maltreatment during childhood and adjustment in young adulthood. *Child Abuse & Neglect, 21,* 617–630.

Fergusson, D. M., Lynskey, M. T., & Horwood, L. J. (1996). Childhood sexual abuse and psychiatric disorders in young adulthood: Part I: The prevalence of sexual abuse and the factors associated with sexual abuse. *Journal of the American Academy of Child and Adolescent Psychiatry, 35,* 1355–1364.

Finkelhor, D. (1984). *Child sexual abuse: New theory and research.* New York: Free Press.

Finkelhor, D. (1988). The trauma of sexual abuse: Two models. In G. E. Wyatt & G. J. Powell (Eds.), *Lasting effects of child sexual abuse* (pp. 61–82). Newbury Park, CA: Sage.

Finkelhor, D. (1990). Early and long-term effects of child sexual abuse: An update. *Professional Psychology: Research and Practice, 21,* 325–330.

Finkelhor, D. (1993). Epidemiological factors in the clinical identification of child sexual abuse. *Child Abuse & Neglect, 17,* 67–70.

Finkelhor, D. (1994). The international epidemiology of child sexual abuse. *Child Abuse & Neglect, 18,* 409–417.

Finkelhor, D., & Baron, L. (1986). High risk children. In D. Finkelhor (Ed.), *A sourcebook on child sexual abuse* (pp. 60–88). Beverly Hills, CA: Sage.

Finkelhor, D., & Berliner, L. (1995). Research on the treatment of sexually abused children: A review and recommendations. *Journal of the American Academy of Child and Adolescent Psychiatry, 34,* 1408–1423.

Finkelhor, D., & Dziuba-Leatherman, J. (1994). Children as victims of violence: A national survey. *Pediatrics, 94,* 413–420.

Finkelhor, D., Hotaling, G., Lewis, I. A., & Smith, C. (1990). Sexual abuse in a national survey of adult men and women. *Child Abuse & Neglect, 14,* 19–28.

Finkelhor, D., & Williams, L. M. (1988). *Nursery crimes: Sexual abuse in day care centres.* Newbury Park, CA: Sage.

Finn, S. E., Hartmann, M., Leon, G. R., & Lawson, L. (1986). Eating disorders and sexual abuse: Lack of confirmation for a clinical hypothesis. *International Journal of Eating Disorders, 5,* 1051–1060.

Fleming, J., Mullen, P. E., & Bammer, G. (1997). A study of potential risk factors for sexual abuse in childhood. *Child Abuse & Neglect, 21,* 49–58.

Fleming, J. M. (1997). Prevalence of childhood sexual abuse in a community sample of Australian women. *Medical Journal of Australia, 166,* 65–68.

Flin, R., Bull, R., Boon, J., & Knox, A. (1992). Children in the witness box. In H. Dent & R. Flin (Eds.), *Children as witnesses.* Chichester, UK: Wiley.

Fowler, F. J., & Mangione, T. W. (1989). *Standardized survey interviewing: Minimizing interviewer-related error.* Newbury Park, CA: Sage.

Fox, K. M., & Gilbert, B. O. (1994). The interpersonal and psychological functioning of women who experienced childhood physical abuse, incest, and parental alcoholism. *Child Abuse & Neglect, 18,* 849–858.

Fredrickson, R. (1992). *Repressed memories: A journey to recovery from sexual abuse.* New York: Simon & Schuster.

Freud, S. (1896). The aetiology of hysteria. In P. Gay (Ed.), *The Freud reader* (pp. 96–111). New York: W. W. Norton.

Freund, K., Watson, R., & Dickey, R. (1990). Does sexual abuse in childhood cause pedophilia?: An exploratory study. *Archives of Sexual Behavior, 19,* 557–568.

Friedrich, W., Beilke, R., & Urquiza, A. (1987). Children from sexually abusive families: A behavioral comparison. *Journal of Interpersonal Violence, 2,* 391–402.

Friedrich, W., Urquiza, A. J., & Beilke, R. L. (1986). Behavior problems in sexually abused young children. *Journal of Pediatric Psychology, 11,* 47–57.

Gershenson, H. P., Musick, J. S., Ruch-Ross, H., Magee, V., Rubino, K. K., & Rosenberg, D. (1989). The prevalence of coercive sexual experience among teenage mothers. *Journal of Interpersonal Violence, 4,* 204–219.

Gomes-Schwartz, B., Horowitz, J. M., Cardarelli, A. P., & Sauzier, M. (1990). *Child sexual abuse: The initial effects.* Newbury Park, CA: Sage.

Goodman, G., Quinn, J., Bottoms, B., & Shaver, P. (1994). *Characteristics of allegations of ritualistic child abuse: Final report to the National Center on Child Abuse and Neglect.* Washington: National Center on Child Abuse and Neglect.

Goodman, G. S., & Clarke-Stewart, A. (1991). Suggestibility in children's testimony: Implications for child sexual abuse investigations. In J. L. Doris (Ed.), *The suggestibility of children's recollections* (pp. 92–105). Washington, DC: American Psychological Association.

Goodman, G. S., Hirschman, J. E., Hepps, D., & Rudy, L. (1991). Children's memory for stressful events. *Merrill Palmer Quarterly, 37,* 109–158.

Goodwin, J. (1985). Post-traumatic symptoms in incest victims. In S. Eth & R. S. Pynoos (Eds.), *Post-traumatic stress disorder in children* (pp. 157–168). Los Angeles, CA: American Psychiatric Association.

Goodyear-Smith, F. (1993). *First do no harm: The sexual abuse industry.* Auckland, NZ: Benton Guy Publishers.

Gorcey, M., Santiago, J. M., & McCall-Perez, F. (1986). Psychological consequences for women sexually abused in childhood. *Social Psychiatry, 21,* 129–133.

Gould, D. A., Stevens, N. G., Ward, N. G., Carlin, A. S., Sowell, H. E., & Gustafson, B. (1994). Self-reported childhood abuse in an adult population in a primary care setting. Prevalence, correlates and associated suicide attempts. *Archives of Family Medicine, 3,* 252–256.

Green, A. H. (1986). True and false allegations of sexual abuse in child custody disputes. *Journal of the American Academy of Child Psychiatry, 25,* 449–456.

Green, A. H. (1993). Child sexual abuse: Immediate and long term effects and intervention. *Journal of the American Academy of Child and Adolescent Psychiatry, 32,* 890–902.

Groves, R. M. (1989). *Survey errors and survey costs.* New York: John Wiley & Sons.

Hall, R. C. W., Tice, L., Beresford, T. P., Wooley, B., & Hall, A. K. (1989). Sexual abuse in patients with anorexia nervosa and bulimia. *Psychosomatics, 30,* 73–79.

Halperin, D. S., Bouvier, P., Jaffe, P. D., Mounoud, R., Pawlak, C. H., Laederach, J., Rey Wicky, H., & Astie, F. (1996). Prevalence of child sexual abuse among adolescents in Geneva: Results of a cross-sectional survey. *British Medical Journal, 312,* 1326–1329.

Hamilton, G. V. (1929). *A research in marriage.* New York: Albert & Charles Boni.

Hanson, R. K. (1990). Characteristics of sex offenders who were sexually abused as children. In R. Langevin (Ed.), *Sex offenders and their victims* (pp. 77–85). Oakville, Ontario: Juniper.

Hanson, R. K., & Slater, S. (1988). Sexual victimization in the history of sexual abusers: A review. *Annals of Sex Research, 1,* 485–499.

Harvey, M. R., & Herman, J. L. (1994). Amnesia, partial amnesia and delayed recall among adult survivors of childhood trauma. *Consciousness and Cognition, 3,* 295–306.

Haugaard, J. J., & Emery, R. E. (1989). Methodological issues in child sexual abuse research. *Child Abuse & Neglect, 13,* 89–100.

Haugaard, J. J., & Reppucci, N. D. (1988). *The sexual abuse of children.* San Francisco: Jossey-Bass.

Henry, B., Moffitt, T. E., Caspi, A., Langley, J., & Silva, P. (1994). On the "remembrance of things past": A longitudinal evaluation of the retrospective method. *Psychological Assessment, 6, 92101.*

Herman, J. (1992). *Trauma and recovery.* New York: Basic Books.

Herman, J. L. (1981). *Father-daughter incest.* Cambridge, MA: Harvard University Press.

Herman, J. L., & Schatzow, E. (1984). Recovery and verification of memories of childhood sexual trauma. *Psychoanalytic Psychology, 4,* 1–14.

Hibbard, R. A., Ingersoll, G. M., & Orr, D. P. (1990). Behavioral risk, emotional risk, and child abuse among adolescents in a nonclinical setting. *Pediatrics, 86,* 896–901.

Hooper, P. D. (1990). Psychological sequelae of sexual abuse in childhood. *British Journal of General Practice, 40,* 29–31.

Hussey, D. L., & Singer, M. (1993). Psychological distress, problem behaviors and family functioning of sexually abused adolescent inpatients. *Journal of the American Academy of Child and Adolescent Psychiatry, 32,* 954–961.

Hyde, C., Bentovim, A., & Monck, E. (1995). Some clinical and methodological implications of a treatment outcome study of sexually abused children. *Child Abuse & Neglect, 11,* 1387–1399.

Jonker, F., & Jonker, B. I. (1997). Effects of ritual abuse: The results of three surveys in the Netherlands. *Child Abuse & Neglect, 21,* 541–556.

Jumper, S. A. (1995). A meta-analysis of the relationship of child sexual abuse to adult psychological adjustment. *Child Abuse & Neglect, 19,* 715–728.

Kearney-Cooke, A. (1988). Group treatment of sexual abuse among women with eating disorders. *Women and Therapy, 7,* 5–22.

Kempe, C. H., Silverman, F. N., Steele, B. F., Droegemueller, W., & Silver, H. K. (1962). The battered child syndrome. *Journal of the American Medical Association, 181,* 17–24.

Kendall-Tackett, K. A., Williams, L. M., & Finkelhor, D. (1993). Impact of sexual abuse on children: A review and synthesis of recent empirical studies. *Psychological Bulletin, 113,* 164–180.

Kinsey, A. C., Pomeroy, W. B., Martin, C. E., & Gebhardt, P. H. (1953). *Sexual behavior in the human female.* Philadelphia: W. B. Saunders.

Kinzl, J. F., Traweger, C., & Biefl, W. (1995). Sexual dysfunctions: Relationship to childhood sexual abuse and early family experiences in a nonclinical sample. *Child Abuse & Neglect, 19,* 785–792.

Kiser, L. J., Ackerman, B. J., Brown, E., Edwards, N. B., McColgan, E., Pugh, R., & Pruitt, D. B. (1988). Post-traumatic stress disorder in young children: A reaction to purported sexual abuse. *Journal of the American Academy of Child and Adolescent Psychiatry, 27,* 645–649.

Kopelman, M. D. (1996). Anomalies of autobiographical memory: Retrograde amnesia, delusional memory, psychogenic amnesia and false memories. In J. D. Read & D. S. Lindsay (Eds.), *Recollections of trauma—Scientific research and clinical practice.* New York: Plenum.

Krugman, S., Mata, L., & Krugman, R. (1992). Sexual abuse and corporal punishment during childhood: A pilot retrospective survey of university students in Costa Rica. *Pediatrics, 90,* 157–161.

La Fontaine, J. S. (1994). *The extent and nature of organised and ritual abuse: Research findings.* London: Department of Health.

Ladwig, G. B., & Anderson, M. D. (1989). Substance abuse in women: Relationship between chemical dependency of women and past reports of physical and/or sexual abuse. *International Journal of Addiction, 24,* 739–754.

Landis, C., Landis, A. T., Bolles, M., Metzger, H. F., Pitts, M. W., D'Esopo, D. A., Moloy, H. C., Kleegman, S. J., & Dickenson, R. L. (1940). *Sex in development.* New York: Paul B. Hoebert.

Langevin, R., Wortzman, G., Wright, P., & Handy, L. (1989). Studies of brain damage and dysfunction in sex offenders. *Annals of Sex Research, 2,* 163–179.

Lanning, K. V. (1989, October 1–11). Satanic, occult, ritualistic crime. A law-enforcement perspective. *Police Chief,* pp. 1–11.

Lindberg, F., & Distad, L. (1985). Survival responses to incest: Adolescents in crisis. *Child Abuse & Neglect, 9,* 521–526.

Lodico, M. A., Gruber, E., & DiClemente, R. J. (1996). Childhood sexual abuse and coercive sex among school-based adolescents in a midwestern state. *Journal of Adolescent Health, 18,* 211–217.

Loftus, E. F. (1993). The reality of repressed memories. *American Psychologist, 48,* 518–37.

Loftus, E. F., Polonsky, S., & Fullilove, M. T. (1994). Memories of childhood sexual abuse: Remembering and repressing. *Psychology of Women Quarterly, 18,* 67–84.

Ludwig, A. M., Brandsma, J. M., Wilbur, C. B., Benfeldt, F., & Jameson, D. G. (1972). The objective study of multiple personality, or are four heads better than one? *Archives of General Psychiatry, 26,* 298–310.

Mannarino, A. P., Cohen, J. A., & Gregor, M. (1989). Emotional and behavioral difficulties in sexually abused girls. *Journal of Family Violence, 4,* 437–451.

Martin, J., Perrott, K., Morris, W., & Romans, S. (in press). Participation in retrospective child sexual abuse research: Beneficial or harmful? In L. Williams & V. Banyard (Eds.), *Trauma and memory: An International Research Conference* (pp. 149–159). Thousand Oaks, CA: Sage.

Martin, J. L., Anderson, J. C., Romans, S. E., Mullen, P. E., & O'Shea, M. (1993). Asking about child sexual abuse: Methodological implications of a two stage survey. *Child Abuse & Neglect, 17,* 383–392.

Martin, M. J., & Walters, J. (1982). Familial correlates of selected types of child abuse and neglect. *Journal of Marriage and the Family, 44,* 267–276.

Masson, J. M. (1985). *The assault on truth: Freud's suppression of the seduction theory.* New York: Penguin.

McDevitt, S. (1996). The impact of news media on child abuse reporting. *Child Abuse & Neglect, 20,* 261–274.

McGain, B., & McKinzey, R. K. (1995). The efficacy of group treatment in sexually abused girls. *Child Abuse & Neglect, 19,* 1157–1169.

McGregor, K. (1994). *Warriors of truth: Adult survivors healing from childhood sexual abuse.* Dunedin, NZ: University of Otago Press.

Melchert, T. P., & Parker, R. L. (1997). Different forms of childhood abuse and memory. *Child Abuse & Neglect, 21,* 125–135.

Merry, S. N., & Andrews, L. K. (1989). Doing research in the real world—A case history and some implications for medical research. *New Zealand Medical Journal, 102,* 351–353.

Miller, B. C., Monson, B. H., & Norton, M. C. (1995). The effects of forced sexual intercourse on white female adolescents. *Child Abuse & Neglect, 19,* 1289–1301.

Miller, D. A. F., & McCluskey-Fawcett, K. (1993). The relationship between childhood sexual abuse and subsequent onset of bulimia nervosa. *Child Abuse & Neglect, 17,* 305–314.

Moeller, T. P., Bachmann, G. A., & Moeller, J. R. (1993). The combined effects of physical, sexual and emotional abuse during childhood, long term health consequences for women. *Child Abuse & Neglect, 17,* 623–640.

Moran, P. B., & Eckenrode, J. (1992). Protective personality characteristics among adolescent victims of maltreatment. *Child Abuse & Neglect, 16,* 743–754.

Mullen, P. E., Martin, J. L., Anderson, J. C., Romans, S. E., & Herbison, G. P. (1993). Childhood sexual abuse and mental health in adult life. *British Journal of Psychiatry, 163,* 721–732.

Mullen, P. E., Martin, J. L., Anderson, J. C., Romans, S. E., & Herbison, G. P. (1994). The effects of child sexual abuse on social, interpersonal and sexual function in adult life. *British Journal of Psychiatry, 165,* 35–47.

Mullen, P. E., Martin, J. L., Anderson, J. C., Romans, S. E., & Herbison, G. P. (1996). The long-term impact of the physical, emotional and sexual abuse of children: A community study. *Child Abuse & Neglect, 20,* 7–21.

Murphy, W. D., & Smith, T. A. (1996). Sex offenders against children. In J. Briere, L. Berliner, J. Bulkley, C. Jenny, & T. Reid (Eds.), *The APSAC handbook on child maltreatment.* Thousand Oaks, CA: Sage.

Nagy, S., Adcock, A. G., & Nagy, M. C. (1994). A comparison of risky health behaviors of sexually active, sexually abused and abstaining adolescents. *Pediatrics, 93,* 570–575.

Nagy, S., DiClemente, R., & Adcock, A. G. (1995). Adverse factors associated with forced sex among southern adolescent girls. *Pediatrics, 96,* 944–946.

Nelson, D. E., Higginson, G. K., & Grant-Worley, J. (1994). Using the Youth Risk Behavior Survey to estimate prevalence of sexual abuse among Oregon high school students. *Journal of School Health, 64,* 413–416.

Nelson, K. (1993). The psychological and social origins of autobiographical memory. *Psychological Science, 4,* 7–14.

Oates, R. K., O'Toole, B. I., Lynch, D. L., Stern, A., & Cooney, G. (1994). Stability and change in outcomes for sexually abused children. *Journal of the American Academy of Child and Adolescent Psychiatry, 33*, 945–953.

Ofshe, R., & Watters, E. (1993, March/April). Making monsters. *Society*, pp. 4–16.

Ofshe, R., & Watters, E. (1994). *Making monsters: False memories, psychotherapy and sexual hysteria.* New York: Scribner's.

Olafson, E., Corwin, D. L., & Summit, R. C. (1993). Modern history of child sexual abuse awareness: Cycles of discovery and suppression. *Child Abuse & Neglect, 17*, 7–24.

Olio, K. A., & Cornell, W. F. (1994). Making meaning not monsters: Reflections on the delayed memory controversy. *Journal of Child Sexual Abuse, 3*, 77–94.

Oppenheimer, R., Howells, K., Palmer, R. L., & Chaloner, D. A. (1985). Adverse sexual experiences in childhood and clinical eating disorders: A preliminary description. *Journal of Psychiatric Research, 19*, 357–361.

Paradise, J. E., Rose, L., Sleeper, L. A., & Nathanson, M. (1994). Behavior, family function, school performance and predictors of persistent disturbance in sexually abused children. *Pediatrics, 93*, 452–459.

Peluso, E., & Putnam, N. (1996). Case study: Sexual abuse of boys by females. *Journal of the American Academy of Child and Adolescent Psychiatry, 35*, 51–54.

Penfold, P. S. (1996). The repressed memory controversy: Is there middle ground? *Canadian Medical Association Journal, 155*, 647–653.

Peters, D. K., & Range, L. M. (1995). Childhood sexual abuse and current suicidality in college women and men. *Child Abuse & Neglect, 19*, 335–341.

Peters, D. S., Wyatt, G. E., & Finkelhor, D. (1986). Prevalence. In D. Finkelhor (Ed.), *A sourcebook on child sexual abuse* (pp. 15–59). Beverly Hills, CA: Sage.

Peters, S. D. (1988). Child sexual assault and later psychological problems. In G. E. Wyatt & G. J. Powell, (Eds.), *Lasting effects of child sexual abuse.* Newbury Park, CA: Sage.

Pickles, A. (1995). Statistical analysis in epidemiology. In F. C. Verhulst & H. M. Koot (Eds.), *The epidemiology of child and adolescent psychopathology* (pp. 104–121). Oxford: Oxford University Press.

Pilkonis, P. A. (1993). Studying the effects of treatment in victims of childhood sexual abuse. *Journal of Interpersonal Violence, 8*, 392–401.

Plunkett, A., & Oates, R. K. (1990). Methodological considerations in research on child sexual abuse. *Paediatric and Perinatal Epidemiology, 4*, 351–360.

Prendergast, M. (1993). *For God, country, and Coca-Cola.* New York: Collier.

Pribor, E. F., & Dinwiddie, S. H. (1992). Psychiatric correlates of incest in childhood. *American Journal of Psychiatry, 149*, 455–463.

Putnam, F. W. (1991). The satanic ritual abuse controversy. *Child Abuse & Neglect, 15*, 175–179.

Putnam, F. W., Guroff, J. J., Silberman, E. K., Barvan, L., & Post, R. M. (1986). The clinical phenomenology of multiple personality disorder: Review of 100 recent cases. *Journal of Clinical Psychiatry, 47*, 285–293.

Reeker, J., Ensing, D., & Elliott, R. (1997). A meta-analytic investigation of group treatment outcomes for sexually abused children. *Child Abuse & Neglect, 21*, 669–680.

Rich, C. L. (1990). Accuracy of adults' reports of abuse in childhood. *American Journal of Psychiatry, 147*, 1389.

Rogers, C. N., & Terry, T. (1984). Clinical interventions with boy victims of sexual abuse. In I. R. Stuart & J. G. Greer (Eds.), *Victims of sexual aggression: Treatment of children, women and men.* New York: Van Nostrand Reinhold.

Romans, S. E., Martin, J. L., Anderson, J. C., O'Shea, M. L., & Mullen, P. F. (1995). Factors that mediate between child sexual abuse and adult psychological outcome. *Psychological Medicine, 25,* 127–142.

Root, M. P., & Fallon, P. (1988). The incidence of victimization experiences in a bulimic sample. *Journal of Interpersonal Violence, 3,* 161–173.

Rorty, M., Yager, J., & Rossotto, E. (1994). Childhood sexual physical and psychological abuse in bulimia nervosa. *American Journal of Psychiatry, 151,* 1122–1126.

Ross, C. A., Anderson, G., Fleisher, W. P., & Norton, G. R. (1991). The frequency of multiple personality disorder amongst psychiatric inpatients. *American Journal of Psychiatry, 148,* 1717–1720.

Rothman, K. J. (1986). *Modern epidemiology.* Boston: Little, Brown.

Rowan, A. B., Foy, D. W., Rodriguez, N., & Ryan, S. (1994). Posttraumatic stress disorder in a clinical sample of adults sexually abused as children. *Child Abuse & Neglect, 18,* 51–61.

Rudy, L., & Goodman, G. S. (1991). Effects of participation on children's reports: Implications for children's testimony. *Developmental Psychology, 27,* 527–538.

Rush, F. (1974). The sexual abuse of children: A feminist point of view. In N. Connell & C. Wilson (Eds.), *Rape: The first sourcebook for women.* New York: New American Library.

Rush, F. (1980). *The best kept secret: Sexual abuse of children.* New York: McGraw-Hill.

Russell, D. E. H. (1986). *The secret trauma: Incest in the lives of girls and women.* New York: Basic Books.

Rutter, M. (1981). *Maternal deprivation reassessed.* Harmondsworth, UK: Penguin.

Rutter, M. (1995). Clinical implications of attachment concepts: Retrospect and prospect. *Journal of Child Psychology and Psychiatry, 36,* 549–571.

Saphira, M. (1985). *For your child's sake: Understanding sexual abuse.* Auckland, NZ: Reed.

Sariola, H., & Uutela, A. (1994). The prevalence of child sexual abuse in Finland. *Child Abuse & Neglect, 18,* 827–835.

Saywitz, K., Goodman, G. S., Nicholas, G., & Moon, S. (1991). Children's memory of a physical examination involving genital touch: Implications for reports of sexual abuse. *Journal of Consulting and Clinical Psychology, 5,* 682–691.

Schacter, D. L. (1996). *Searching for memory: The brain, the mind, and the past.* New York: Basic Books.

Schreiber, F. (1973). *Sybil.* Chicago: Regency.

Schwarz, N., & Sudman, S. (1992). *Context effects in social and psychological research.* New York: Springer-Verlag.

Scott, D. (1995). The social construction of child sexual abuse: Debates about definitions and the politics of prevalence. *Psychiatry, Psychology and Law, 2,* 117–126.

Scott, K. D. (1992). Childhood sexual abuse: Impact on a community's mental health status. *Child Abuse & Neglect, 16,* 285–295.

Siegel, J. M., Sorenson, S. B., Golding, J. M., Burnam, M. A., & Stein, J. A. (1987). The prevalence of childhood sexual assault: The Los Angeles epidemiologic catchment area project. *American Journal of Epidemiology, 126,* 1141–1153.

Silverman, A. B., Reinherz, H. Z., & Giaconia, R. M. (1996). The long-term sequelae of child and adolescent abuse: A longitudinal community study. *Child Abuse & Neglect, 20,* 709–723.

Simpson, A. E. (1988). Vulnerability and the age of female consent: Legal innovation and its effect on prosecutions for rape in eighteenth-century London. In G. S. Rousseau & R. Porter (Eds.), *Sexual underworlds of the Enlightenment* (pp. 181–205). Chapel Hill: University of North Carolina Press.

Sirles, E. A., Smith, J. A., & Kusama, H. (1989). Psychiatric status of intrafamilial child sexual abuse victims. *Journal of the American Academy of Child and Adolescent Psychiatry, 28,* 225–229.

Smith, D., Pearce, L., Pringle, M., & Caplan, R. (1995). Adults with a history of child sexual abuse: Evaluation of a pilot therapy service. *British Medical Journal, 310,* 1175–1178.

Spaccarelli, S. (1994). Stress, appraisal, and coping in child sexual abuse: A theoretical and empirical review. *Psychological Bulletin, 116,* 340–362.

Spaccarelli, S., & Kim, S. (1995). Resilience criteria and factors associated with resilience in sexually abused girls. *Child Abuse & Neglect, 19,* 1171–1182.

Spanos, N. P. (1996). *Multiple identities & false memories: A sociocognitive perspective.* Washington, DC: American Psychological Association.

Spiegel, D. (1994) Multiple personality as a post-traumatic stress disorder. *Psychiatric Clinics of North America, 7,* 101–110.

Spiegel, D., & Cardèna, E. (1991). Disintegrated experience: The dissociative disorders revisited. *Journal of Abnormal Psychology, 100,* 366–378.

Springs, F. E., & Friedrich, W. N. (1992). Health risk behaviors and medical sequelae of childhood sexual abuse. *Mayo Clinic Proceedings, 67,* 527–532.

Squire, L. (1989). On the course of forgetting in very long-term memory. *Journal of Experimental Psychology: Learning, Memory and Cognition, 15,* 241–245.

Steiger, M., & Zanko, M. (1990). Sexual trauma among eating disordered, psychiatric and normal female groups. *Journal of Interpersonal Violence, 5,* 74–86.

Stein, J. A., Golding, J. M., Siegel, J. M., Burnam, M. A., & Sorenson, S. B. (1988). Long term sequelae of child sexual abuse. In G. E. Wyatt & G. J. Powell (Eds.), *Lasting effects of child sexual abuse* (pp. 135–154). Newbury Park, CA: Sage.

Stern, A. E., Lynch, D. L., Oates, R. K., O'Toole, B. I., & Cooney, G. (1995). Self esteem, depression, behavior and family functioning in sexually abused children. *Journal of Child Psychology and Psychiatry, 36,* 1077–1089.

Steward, M. S., Steward, D., Farquhar, L., Myers, J. E. B., Reinhart, M., Welker, J., Joyle, N., Driskill, J., & Morgan, J. (1996). Interviewing young children about body touch and handling. *Monographs of the Society for Research in Child Development, 61,* 204–214.

Summit, R. (1988). Hidden victims, hidden pain in societal avoidance of child sexual abuse. In G. E. Wyatt and G. J. Powell (Eds.), *Lasting effects of child sexual abuse.* Beverley Hills, CA: Sage.

Summit, R. C. (1983). The child sexual accommodation syndrome. *Child Abuse & Neglect, 7,* 177–193.

Susser, M. (1973). *Causal thinking in the health sciences: Concepts and strategies of epidemiology.* New York: Oxford University Press.

Terr, L. C. (1991). Childhood traumas: An outline and overview. *American Journal of Psychiatry, 148,* 10–20.

Terr, L. C. (1994). *Unchained memories: True stories of traumatic memories, lost and found.* New York: Basic Books.

Trepper, T. S., & Barrett, M. J. (1989). *Systemic treatment of incest: A therapeutic handbook.* New York: Brunner/Mazel.

van der Kolk, B. A. (1994). The body keeps the score: Memory and the evolving psychobiology of PTSD. *Harvard Review of Psychiatry, 1,* 253–265.

Vanderlinden, J., Vandereycken, W., van Dyck, R., & Vertommen, H. (1993). Dissociative experiences and trauma in eating disorders. *International Journal of Eating Disorders, 13,* 187–193.

Von Dadelszen, J. (1987). *Sexual abuse study: An examination of the histories of sexual abuse among girls currently in the care of the Department of Social Welfare.* Wellington, NZ: Department of Social Welfare.

Wakefield, H., & Underwager, R. (1992). Recovered memories of alleged sexual abuse: Lawsuits against parents. *Behavioural Sciences and the Law, 10,* 483–507.

Waterman, J., & Kelly, R. J. (1993). Mediators of effects on children: What enhances optimal functioning and promotes healing? In J. Waterman, R. J. Kelly, M. K. Oliver, & J. McCord (Eds.), *Behind the playground walls: Sexual abuse in preschools.* (pp. 222–239). New York: Guilford.

Watkins, W., & Bentovim, A. (1992). The sexual abuse of male children and adolescents: A review of current research. *Journal of Child Psychology and Psychiatry, 33,* 197–248.

Wellman, M. M. (1993). Child sexual abuse and gender differences: Attitudes and prevalence. *Child Abuse & Neglect, 17,* 539–547.

Whipple, E. E., & Webster-Stratton, C. (1991). The role of parental stress in physically abusive families. *Child Abuse & Neglect, 15,* 279–291.

Williams, L. M. (1994). Recall of childhood trauma: A prospective study of women's memories of child sexual abuse. *Journal of Consulting and Clinical Psychology, 62,* 1167–1176.

Williams, L. M. (1995). Recovered memories of abuse in women with documented child sexual victimization histories. *Journal of Traumatic Stress, 8,* 649–673.

Winfield I., George, L. K., Swartz, M., & Blazer, D. G. (1990). Sexual assault and psychiatric disorders among a community sample of women. *American Journal of Psychiatry, 147,* 335–341.

Winsgrad, E., & Reisser, U. (1992). *Affects and accuracy in recall: Studies of flashback memories.* New York: Cambridge University Press.

Wonderlich, S. A., Brewerton, T. D., Jocic, Z., Dansky, B. S., & Abbott, D. W. (1997). Relationship of childhood sexual abuse and eating disorders. *Journal of the American Academy of Child and Adolescent Psychiatry, 36,* 1107–1115.

Wonderlich, S. A., Wilsnack, R. W., Wilsnack, S. C., & Harris, T. R. (1996). Childhood sexual abuse and bulimic behavior in a nationally representative sample. *American Journal of Public Health, 86,* 1082–1086.

Wyatt, G. E., Guthrie, D., & Notgrass, C. M. (1992). Differential effects of women's child sexual abuse and subsequent sexual revictimization. *Journal of Consulting and Clinical Psychology, 60,* 167–173.

Yates, A. (1978). *Sex without shame.* New York: William Morrow.

Zierler, S., Feingold, L., Laufer, D., Velentgas, P., Kantrowitz-Gordon, I., & Mayer, K. (1991). Adult survivors of childhood sexual abuse and subsequent risk of HIV infection. *American Journal of Public Health, 81,* 572–575.

INDEX

125

ABOUT THE AUTHORS

David M. Fergusson is Associate Professor of the Christchurch School of Medicine and Executive Director of the Christchurch Health and Development Study. He has an extremely strong background in research and spans multiple disciplines, both in his training and in the type of research he conducts. He has published extensively and is recognized internationally for writing a large number of high-quality articles on child and adolescent adjustment and clinical dysfunction. He has been the recipient of major grants, is professionally very active, and is involved with various conferences and boards.

Paul E. Mullen is Foundation Professor of Forensic Psychiatry at Monash University, and Director of the Victorian Institute of Forensic Mental Health. He has completed advanced degrees in medicine and forensics. A highly accomplished author who is very active and visible professionally, he has a superb publication record in psychiatry, medicine, and health.

Both authors, although working in Australia and New Zealand, have published widely in English-speaking countries and journals. Their publication records in sources in the United States and Great Britain have established their credentials, seniority in the field, and expertise on the topic of child sexual abuse.